The series Lecture Notes in Computer Science (LNCS), including its subseries Lecture Notes in Artificial Intelligence (LNAI) and Lecture Notes in Bioinformatics (LNBI), has established itself as a medium for the publication of new developments in computer science and information technology research, teaching, and education.

LNCS enjoys close cooperation with the computer science R & D community, the series counts many renowned academics among its volume editors and paper authors, and collaborates with prestigious societies. Its mission is to serve this international community by providing an invaluable service, mainly focused on the publication of conference and workshop proceedings and postproceedings. LNCS commenced publication in 1973.

Huawei Huang · Songlin He · Junbin Fang ·
Liang-Jie Zhang
Editors

# Blockchain – ICBC 2026

9th International Conference
Held as Part of the Smart Computing Frontier, SCF 2026
Kuala Lumpur, Malaysia, August 22–25, 2026, Proceedings

Springer

*Editors*
Huawei Huang
Sun Yat-sen University
Zhuhai, Guangdong, China

Songlin He
Southwest Jiaotong University
Chengdu, China

Junbin Fang
Jinan University
Guangzhou, China

Liang-Jie Zhang
Shenzhen University
Shenzhen, China

ISSN 0302-9743 ISSN 1611-3349 (electronic)
Lecture Notes in Computer Science
ISBN 978-3-032-36765-5 ISBN 978-3-032-36766-2 (eBook)
https://doi.org/10.1007/978-3-032-36766-2



This Springer imprint is published by the registered company Springer Nature Switzerland AG
The registered company address is: Gewerbestrasse 11, 6330 Cham, Switzerland

If disposing of this product, please recycle the paper.

# Preface

The International Conference on Blockchain (ICBC) aims to provide an international forum for both researchers and industry practitioners to exchange the latest fundamental advances in the state-of-the-art technologies and best practices of blockchain, as well as emerging standards and research topics which will define the future of blockchain.

ICBC 2026 was a member of the Smart Computing Frontier (SCF). SCF 2026 had the following 10 collocated service-oriented sister conferences: 2026 International Conference on Web Services (ICWS 2026), 2026 International Conference on Cloud Computing (CLOUD 2026), 2026 International Conference on Services Computing (SCC 2026), 2026 International Conference on Big Data (BigData 2026), 2026 International Conference on AI & Multimodal Services (AIMS 2026), 2026 International Conference on Metaverse (METAVERSE 2026), 2026 International Conference on Internet of Things (ICIOT 2026), 2026 International Conference on Cognitive Computing (ICCC 2026), 2026 International Conference on Edge Computing (EDGE 2026), and 2026 International Conference on Blockchain (ICBC 2026).

This volume presents the accepted papers of the 2026 International Conference on Blockchain (ICBC 2026), held in Kuala Lumpur, Malaysia during August 22–25, 2026. For this conference, each paper was single-blind reviewed by three independent members of the International Program Committee. After carefully evaluating the submissions' originality and quality, we accepted 7 papers from 21 submissions.

We are pleased to thank the authors whose submissions and participation made this conference possible. We also want to express our thanks to the Organizing Committee and Program Committee members, for their dedication in helping to organize the conference and for reviewing the submissions. We owe special thanks to the keynote speakers for their impressive speeches.

Finally, we would like to thank operations team members Jing Zeng, Sheng He, Yishuang Ning, and Zhuolin Mei for their excellent work in organizing this conference. We look forward to your future great contributions as a volunteer, author, and conference participant in the fast-growing worldwide services innovations community.

July 2026

Huawei Huang
Songlin He
Junbin Fang
Liang-Jie Zhang

# Organization

## Honorary Chair

| | |
|---|---|
| Hai Jin | Huazhong University of Science and Technology, China |

## General Chairs

| | |
|---|---|
| Kai Lei | Peking University, China |
| R. K. Shyamasundar | Indian Institute of Technology Bombay, India |

## Program Chairs

| | |
|---|---|
| Huawei Huang | Sun Yat-sen University, China |
| Songlin He | Southwest Jiaotong University, China |
| Junbin Fang | Jinan University, China |

## Smart Computing Frontier (SCF 2026)

## General Chairs

| | |
|---|---|
| Ali Arsanjani | Google, USA |
| Wu Chou | Essenlix Corporation, USA |

## Coordinating Program Chair

| | |
|---|---|
| Liang-Jie Zhang | Shenzhen University, China |

## CFO and International Affairs Chair



## Operation Committee



## Steering Committee



## ICBC 2026 Program Committee

# Conference Sponsor – Services Society

The Services Society (S2) is a non-profit professional organization that has been created to promote worldwide research and technical collaboration in services innovations among academia and industrial professionals. Its members are volunteers from industry and academia with common interests. S2 is registered in the USA as a "501(c) organization", which means that it is an American tax-exempt nonprofit organization. S2 collaborates with other professional organizations to sponsor or co-sponsor conferences and to promote an effective services curriculum in colleges and universities. S2 initiates and promotes a "Services University" program worldwide to bridge the gap between industrial needs and university instruction.

The Services Sector accounted for 79.5% of the GDP of the USA in 2016. The Services Society has formed 5 Special Interest Groups (SIGs) to support technology- and domain-specific professional activities.

- Special Interest Group on Services Computing (SIG-SC)
- Special Interest Group on Big Data (SIG-BD)
- Special Interest Group on Cloud Computing (SIG-CLOUD)
- Special Interest Group on Artificial Intelligence (SIG-AI)
- Special Interest Group on Metaverse (SIG-Metaverse)

# About the Smart Computing Frontier (SCF)

As the founding member of the Smart Computing Frontier (SCF), the first **International Conference on Web Services (ICWS)** was held in June 2003 in Las Vegas, USA. Meanwhile, the First International Conference on Web Services - Europe 2003 (ICWS-Europe 2003) was held in Germany in October 2003. ICWS-Europe 2003 was an extended event of the 2003 International Conference on Web Services (ICWS 2003) in Europe. In 2004, ICWS-Europe was changed to the European Conference on Web Services (ECOWS), which was held in Erfurt, Germany.

Sponsored by the Services Society and Springer, SCF 2018 and SCF 2019 were held successfully on June 25 – June 30, 2018, in Seattle, USA, and on June 25 – June 30, 2019, in San Diego, USA. SCF 2020 and SCF 2021 were held successfully online with a satellite session in Shenzhen, China. SCF 2022 and 2023 were held successfully on December 10–14, 2022 and on September 23–26, 2023, in Hawaii, USA. SCF 2024 was held successfully on November 16–19, 2024, in Bangkok, Thailand. SCF 2025 was successfully held on September 25–30, 2025, in Hong Kong, China. To celebrate its 24th birthday, SCF 2026 was held on **August 22–25, 2026, in Kuala Lumpur, Malaysia**.

In the past 23 years, the ICWS community has expanded from Web engineering innovations to scientific research for the whole services industry. Service delivery platforms have been expanded to mobile platforms, the Internet of Things, cloud computing, and edge computing. The services ecosystem has gradually been enabled, value-added, and intelligence embedded through enabling technologies such as big data, artificial intelligence, and cognitive computing. In the coming years, all transactions with multiple parties involved will be transformed into blockchain and metaverse.

Based on technology trends and best practices in the field, the Smart Computing Frontier (SCF) will continue serving as the conference umbrella's code name for all services-related conferences. SCF 2026 defined the future of New ABCDE (AI, Blockchain, Cloud, BigData & IOT) and entered the 5G for Services Era. **The theme of SCF 2026 was Agentic AI as a Service (AAIaaS).** We are very proud to announce that SCF 2026's 10 co-located theme topic conferences all centered around "services", with each focusing on exploring different themes (web-based services, cloud-based services, Big Data-based services, services innovation lifecycle, AI-driven ubiquitous services, blockchain-driven trust service ecosystems, industry-specific services and applications, and emerging service-oriented technologies).

- **Bigger Platform:** The 10 collocated conferences (SCF 2026) were sponsored by the Services Society, which is the world-leading not-for-profit organization (501(c)(3)) dedicated to the service of more than 30,000 worldwide Services Computing researchers and practitioners. A bigger platform means bigger opportunities for all volunteers, authors, and participants. Meanwhile, Springer provided sponsorship of the best paper awards and other professional activities. All the 10 conference proceedings of SCF 2026 were published by Springer and indexed in the **ISI Conference Proceedings Citation Index (included in Web of Science), Engineering**

**Index EI (Compendex and Inspec databases), DBLP, Google Scholar, IO-Port, MathSciNet, Scopus, and ZBlMath.**

- **Brighter Future:** While celebrating the 2026 version of ICWS, SCF 2026 highlighted the International Conference on AI and Multimodal Services (AIMS 2026) to build the fundamental infrastructure for enabling AIGC services ecosystems. It will also lead our community members to create their own brighter future.
- **Better Model:** SCF 2026 continued to leverage the invented Conference Blockchain Model (CBM) to innovate the organizing practices for all the 10 theme conferences. Senior researchers in the field are welcome to submit proposals to serve as CBM Ambassador for an individual conference to start better interactions during your leadership role in organizing future SCF conferences.

We look forward to your great contributions as a volunteer, author, and conference participant as part of the fast-growing worldwide services innovations community. If you would like to contribute to SCF 2026 as a leading volunteer or try the new Conference Blockchain Model, please feel free to contact us to become a conference volunteer. For other queries or questions, please feel free to visit our conference websites and find contact information on SCF 2026.

All the invited talks and paper presentations of SCF 2020, SCF 2021, and SCF 2022 are open to all Services Society community members for free. You can watch all presentations through SCF 365.

# Contents

# Research Track

# A Serverless Destination Verification System for Cold Wallets Using Smart Contracts

Tomoki Orihara(✉) and Kazumasa Omote

University of Tsukuba, 1-1-1 Tennodai, Tsukuba, Ibaraki 305-8573, Japan
s2620544@u.tsukuba.ac.jp

**Abstract.** Although cold wallets are highly recommended for secure crypto asset management, they are vulnerable to Man-in-the-Mobile (MitMo) attacks where malware on online devices tampers with destination addresses. Conventional countermeasures rely on visually verifying complex alphanumeric addresses, which fails against sophisticated attacks using visually similar addresses. To address this, this study proposes a serverless cold wallet system that prevents address tampering by adapting the BIP 70 Payment Protocol using smart contracts, thereby eliminating server operational costs for service providers. In this system, a Certificate Authority signs data mapping an address to a domain name, which is registered on a smart contract. During transactions, the cold wallet verifies this data and displays the human-readable domain name, enabling users to safely authorize transactions even if the online device is compromised. The effectiveness of the method is demonstrated through a prototype implementation using Android devices and the Sepolia testnet.

**Keywords:** Cold Wallet · Man-in-the-Mobile Attack · Blockchain

## 1 Introduction

In recent years, crypto assets based on blockchain technology [12] have become widespread as a new means of transaction. In the security of crypto assets, the management of private keys, which enable the transfer of assets, is a paramount issue. In particular, the use of a cold wallet, which manages keys in an offline environment, is recommended when prioritizing security. However, when conducting transactions using a cold wallet, it is necessary to connect with an online device such as a PC to broadcast the transaction, and there is a risk that data may be tampered with while passing through this online device.

A particularly serious threat is the tampering of destination addresses. Even if a user enters the correct destination address on an online device, it may be secretly replaced with an attacker's address if the online device is infected with malware. In fact, there was a reported case [4] where 3 Bitcoins (equivalent to $36,000 at the time) were stolen between 2018 and 2019 by "Clipsa," malware


H. Huang et al. (Eds.): ICBC 2026, LNCS 16959, pp. 3–16, 2027.
https://doi.org/10.1007/978-3-032-36766-2_1

that replaces destination addresses. Furthermore, large-scale attacks using similar addresses have occurred in recent years, drastically increasing the financial damages [11]. Since confirmed transactions cannot be reversed, if a user signs a transaction without noticing the tampered destination address, their assets will be permanently lost.

As a conventional countermeasure, the method of displaying the destination address on the cold wallet's screen for visual confirmation by the user has been employed [2,6]. However, it is difficult for humans to accurately verify the validity of an address consisting of a complex sequence of alphanumeric characters.

Therefore, in this study, we construct a novel cold wallet system that can safely retrieve and verify destination addresses even in untrusted environments where online devices are controlled by malware. Specifically, this system adapts the concept of signed destination verification from the BIP 70 Payment Protocol [1] into a serverless destination registry on a smart contract, eliminating the traditionally required payment request server. The traditional BIP 70 mechanism required service providers to maintain and manage a secure payment request server, posing challenges related to operational costs and the risk of server attacks. In contrast, our proposed method adopts an approach where verification data and digital signatures are registered and published on a smart contract in advance. Consequently, while reducing the server operational burden and infrastructure maintenance costs for service providers, we have realized a system that verifies the consistency with the transaction and the correspondence between human-readable strings (domains) and addresses on the cold wallet, thereby safely and reliably detecting and preventing destination address tampering even when operating through a compromised online device.

Finally, we implemented and evaluated the system using an Android device and the Sepolia testnet, demonstrating its effectiveness and practicality.

## 2 Preliminaries

### 2.1 Crypto Assets and Cold Wallets

Crypto assets are digital currencies based on Peer-to-Peer (P2P) networks and cryptography, without a specific central administrator. Representative crypto assets include Bitcoin and Ethereum. The validity of transactions in crypto assets is guaranteed by digital signatures using the private key corresponding to the sender's address. These transaction records are recorded on a distributed ledger called a blockchain, which has extremely high tamper resistance.

However, this robust tamper resistance results in irreversibility, making it difficult to cancel a transaction once it is approved by the network. Even if an erroneous or fraudulent remittance occurs, it is impossible to recover the assets; therefore, the authenticity of the transaction is crucial in the security of crypto assets.

Methods for managing private keys include hot wallets, which are connected to the Internet, and cold wallets, which manage keys in a physically isolated offline environment. While the former offers high convenience, it is constantly exposed to the risk of attacks via the network. In contrast, cold wallets can physically block attacks from external networks, and are widely considered the most secure management method [13].

### 2.2 Smart Contracts

Smart contracts are automated programs that run on the virtual machine on Ethereum (Ethereum Virtual Machine). Due to the characteristics of the blockchain, tampering with recorded code or data is extremely difficult, providing a mechanism to execute predetermined processes without third-party intervention.

### 2.3 BIP 70: Payment Protocol

BIP 70 [1] is a standard designed to improve the payment process in Bitcoin. It is a mechanism in which a trusted third party attaches a signature to a payment request created by a service provider, which includes the destination address, remittance amount, expiration date, etc., and the hardware wallet verifies it. However, the specification lacks explicit instructions to compare the signed data with the destination address of the transaction. Furthermore, in actual operation, because the service provider needs to generate a digitally signed payment request for every transaction, they are required to maintain and manage a secure server, making infrastructure costs and server security management major issues.

### 2.4 QR Code

The QR code is a two-dimensional code suitable for data transfer between physically isolated environments [10]. Its data capacity in the largest Version 40 is 7,089 characters in numeric mode, 4,296 characters in alphanumeric mode, 2,953 bytes in binary mode, and 1,817 characters in Kanji mode, making it possible to transmit a diverse and large amount of data.

### 2.5 Man-in-the-Mobile (MitMo) Attack

In contrast to traditional Man-in-the-Middle (MitM) attacks, which primarily involve eavesdropping and tampering on communication paths, Man-in-the-Mobile (MitMo) attacks target the mobile device itself [5]. This threat has expanded with the transition from PCs to mobile devices, and in the Android OS, there have been reported cases of device compromise through methods such as repackaging attacks [15], which inject malicious code into legitimate applications. Malware that infiltrates the device through such attacks may execute malicious processes in areas undetectable by the user, posing the risk of creating unintended transactions.

# 3 Related Work

## 3.1 Research on the Signature Process of Cold Wallets

Khan et al. [9] proposed a cold wallet system employing QR codes for communication between two Android devices, successfully reducing the risk of private key leakage by physically isolating the cold wallet from the network. However, their research primarily focuses on the secure management of private keys and does not provide countermeasures against scenarios where the destination address is tampered with on an online device by malware.

## 3.2 Research on Address Tampering

Garba et al. [7] revealed that approximately 54% of Bitcoin addresses published on the Web rely on insecure HTTP communication, highlighting the risk that the display itself could be tampered with via a Man-in-the-Middle (MitM) attack. Furthermore, even if an address is acquired safely, a risk of tampering within the device still exists. Ivanov et al. [8] demonstrated the threat of "EthClipper," malware that intercepts the clipboard to substitute the legitimate address with a visually similar one (matching up to 10 characters in total at the beginning and end), pointing out that detection through human visual confirmation is extremely difficult. Although clipboard monitoring tools and strict visual confirmation are recommended as countermeasures, monitoring tools cannot prevent attacks that bypass the clipboard. Furthermore, visual confirmation relies heavily on the user's attentiveness, failing to comprehensively guarantee systemic security.

## 3.3 Research on Address Authentication

Ateniese et al. [3] proposed "Certified Bitcoins," a system where a trusted certificate authority (CA) guarantees identity by generating an address through an interactive protocol. However, their method requires upgrading the software of all participating nodes in the network to incorporate the address verification logic. In contrast, our proposed system operates entirely at the application layer. By leveraging a smart contract constructed on top of the existing blockchain infrastructure, the proposed verification mechanism can be achieved merely by updating the client-side wallet software. Consequently, because there is no need to modify the underlying network protocols, the barrier to adoption is fundamentally lower.

# 4 Proposed Method

## 4.1 Overview

This system is broadly composed of two stages: a "Registration Phase" and a "Payment Phase". In the Registration Phase, preparations are made to guarantee the validity of the service provider's address information, and in the Payment Phase, tampering is detected using a cold wallet.

### 4.2 Registration Phase

The processing flow of the Registration Phase is shown in Fig. 1.

(1) The service provider sends information including its domain name and destination address to the CA and requests a signature.
(2) The CA verifies the validity of the transmitted data and generates a digital signature.
(3) The CA returns the signature to the service provider.
(4) The service provider registers the received signature and the original data as a set in the smart contract and publishes them.

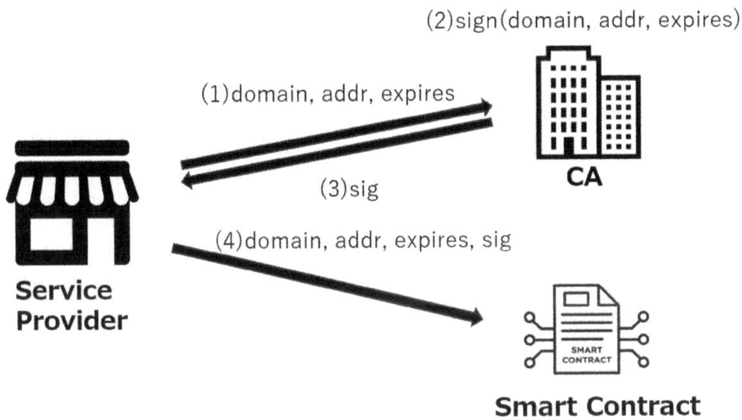


**Fig. 1.** Processing flow of the Registration Phase

### 4.3 Payment Phase

The processing flow of the Payment Phase is shown in Fig. 2.

(1) The online device requests payment data.
(2) The data is retrieved from the smart contract.
(3) A transaction $tx$ is created on the online device.
(4) The online device transfers the constructed $tx$ and the payment request data to the cold wallet.
(5) After checking that the signature has not expired, the cold wallet verifies the $sig$. Simultaneously, it checks whether the address guaranteed by the signature matches the destination in $tx$.
(6) After displaying the *domain* on the screen and obtaining the user's approval, a signature for $tx$ is generated.
(7) The signed $tx$ is returned to the online device.
(8) The $tx$ is broadcast.

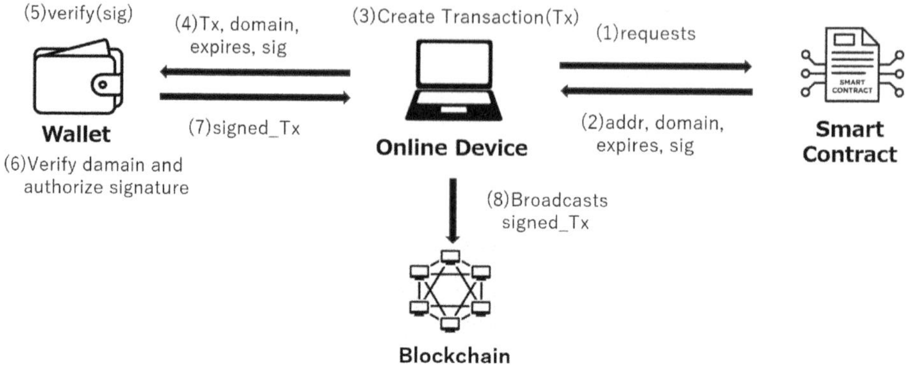


**Fig. 2.** Processing flow of the Payment Phase

### 4.4 System Components

The roles of each component constituting this system are shown below.

1. **Cold Wallet**: A user device operated in an offline environment physically isolated from external networks, responsible for managing the private keys associated with crypto assets. It is defined as a trusted component that is not compromised by attackers. As hardware, it is equipped with a camera for reading data and an interface for displaying the read information.
2. **Online Device**: A user device such as a PC or smartphone operating in an online environment. Considering the possibility of being under an attacker's control due to malware infection or other threats, it is treated as an untrusted component. Similar to the cold wallet, it is equipped with a camera for reading data and an interface for inputting and presenting information as hardware.
3. **Certificate Authority (CA)**: A trusted third-party organization that strictly verifies the identity of the service provider and examines the validity of the presented domain name (*domain*) and receiving address (*addr*).

In this study, the term "domain" refers to a human-readable identifier such as a DNS domain name or blockchain naming identifier (e.g., ENS).

### 4.5 Threat Model

In this study, we assume Man-in-the-Middle (MitM) attacks and Man-in-the-Mobile (MitMo) attacks, where an attacker intervenes in the communication path or relaying devices during the crypto asset remittance process to illegally manipulate data, as the primary threats. Specifically, we assume a threat where, in the process from acquiring the destination address to signing the transaction, the destination address is swapped with an attacker's address unintended by the user on the network or the online device.

### 4.6 Notation

In this paper, we use the notations shown in Table 1.

**Table 1.** Notation

| Symbol | Description |
|---|---|
| $\dashrightarrow$ (Dashed line) | Image transfer using a camera |
| $\longrightarrow$ (Solid line) | Network communication |
| *addr* | Destination address |
| *domain* | Domain name |
| *expires* | Expiration date |
| *sig* | Digital signature |
| *tx* | Transaction |

### 4.7 Preparations

To realize secure remittance processing in this proposed method, the following preparations are required. The CA is assumed to have generated its cryptographic key pair in advance, and the corresponding public key is pre-installed or securely registered in the cold wallet.

**Dataset Creation.** The service provider generates a dataset consisting of its human-readable domain name *domain*, destination address *addr*, and the expiration time of the signature *expires*.

**Digital Signature Generation.** The *domain* and *addr* are sent to the CA. The CA generates a digital signature $sig(domain, addr, expires)$ for the generated dataset.

**Registration in the Smart Contract.** The service provider registers the *domain*, *addr*, *expires*, and the digital signature *sig* in the smart contract.

### 4.8 Payment Flow

The flow of the proposed method is shown in Fig. 3.

**Retrieval of Payment Request Data and Transaction Creation.** At the start of the transaction, the online device (sender) references the target smart contract using the *domain* as a key and directly retrieves the latest payment request data ($addr, expires, sig$) linked to the service provider's *domain*. Based on the retrieved data and the remittance amount entered by the user, the online device constructs a transaction *tx* for the remittance.

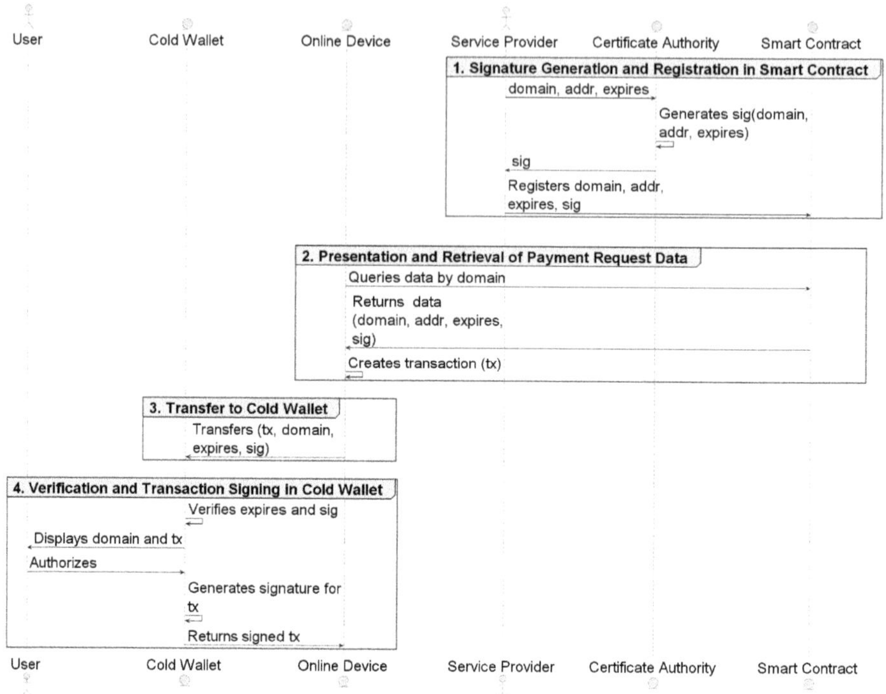


**Fig. 3.** Flow of the proposed method

**Data Transfer to the Cold Wallet.** The online device transfers the created transaction data *tx* and the information necessary for verification (*domain*, *expires*, *sig*) to the cold wallet via a QR code.

**Verification Process on the Cold Wallet.** Upon scanning the QR code, the cold wallet executes the following verification process in an offline environment to prevent address tampering by Man-in-the-Mobile attacks or similar threats. First, as a signature verification, it verifies the signature *sig* using a previously held public key, confirming that the correspondence between the *addr* and *domain* included in *tx* is guaranteed by a legitimate CA. It also evaluates *expires* using its internal clock to check the expiration date of the signature.

**User Approval and Transaction Signing.** After all systematic verifications succeed, the cold wallet displays the human-readable *domain*, remittance amount, and expiration date on the screen. The user visually confirms these details instead of the complex *addr*, and authorizes the signature only when they determine the destination is correct. The signed transaction is once again broadcast to the network via the online device.

# 5 Implementation and Evaluation

To verify the feasibility and effectiveness of the proposed method, we implemented a prototype based on the system configuration shown in Fig. 3.

## 5.1 Environment

The cold wallet and online device were implemented as Android applications, and Kotlin was adopted as the development language. A Google Pixel 9a (Android API Level 36) was used as the operating environment for the cold wallet, utilizing its touch display for data input and its built-in camera for scanning QR codes. However, the online device was implemented using an Android emulator (Android API Level 36) running on a PC.

In the emulator environment, the PC's built-in camera and display were used as substitutes for a physical device's camera and touch display, respectively.

The CA was constructed as a Web application using Java and the Spring Boot framework, and was implemented virtually within the PC. In a production deployment, the CA is assumed to be an organizationally managed service under the standard PKI model. Unlike conventional BIP70-style payment request servers, the CA in the proposed method is only involved during registration and does not participate in per-transaction payment request generation. The HTTP protocol was used for communication with the CA.

Additionally, Sepolia, an Ethereum test network, was used as the storage destination for the verification data. The connection to the Sepolia testnet was established via a public RPC endpoint.

## 5.2 Implementation Details

**Implementation of Address Registration and Signature Generation Process.** We implemented a process where a service provider links their domain name to their destination address. Specifically, the service provider generates a data structure combining the domain name (e.g., merchant.eth) registered on the smart contract, the corresponding address (addr), and the data's expiration date (expires), and sends it to the CA.

On the CA side, an ECDSA signature ($sig$) is generated for this data using the private key of the management server. The generated $\{domain, addr, expires, sig\}$ is deployed onto the smart contract.

**Implementation of QR Code Communication and Offline Verification.** On the cold wallet side, we implemented the logic to restore data from a QR code acquired via the camera and verify its validity offline. With this implementation, even if the online device is compromised by malware and the address within the QR code is rewritten to that of an attacker, the attack is detected on the cold wallet side due to a signature inconsistency.

**Security Verification Against Address Tampering.** To evaluate security effectiveness, we simulated two attack scenarios assuming the online device is compromised by malware.

In Scenario 1, only the address within the payment QR code is replaced with the attacker's address. When the cold wallet scans this QR code, the offline verification logic detects the cryptographic mismatch between the address and the signature. Consequently, a signature verification error automatically aborts the transaction generation, blocking the unauthorized transfer.

In Scenario 2, the entire QR code dataset is replaced with a malicious domain (`attacker.eth`) and its corresponding address pair legitimately obtained from a CA. Although the internal cryptographic verification passes due to the valid signature, the cold wallet displays the verified domain name (`attacker.eth`) instead of a complex address. This allows the user to visually recognize the discrepancy with the intended payee (`merchant.eth`) and manually reject the transaction.

Simulation results confirmed that the system successfully detected and defended against the attacks in both scenarios.

### 5.3 Performance Evaluation

To evaluate the operational cost and practicality of this system, we measured the cost required for registration in the smart contract and the execution time required for the address resolution process on the online device.

**Registration Process to the Smart Contract.** To evaluate the practicality when a service provider deploys verification data (domain name, destination address, expiration date, and signature) to the smart contract, we measured the cost required for registration on the Sepolia testnet.

As a result of the measurement, the gas fee required for a single data registration was approximately 0.000082 ETH.

**Measurement of Execution Time.** To evaluate the response performance of this system, we measured the time required from when the online device sends a request to the smart contract until domain resolution is completed 15 times, and calculated its average value. The measurement results are shown in Table 2.

**Table 2.** Measurement results of execution time

| Processing Item | Time (ms) (Mean $\pm$ SD) |
|---|---|
| Smart contract call | $216 \pm 20$ |
| Domain resolution (total) | $222 \pm 18$ |

# 6 Discussion

## 6.1 Considerations on Practicality

The greatest practical advantage of this method lies in achieving both a reduction in infrastructure management costs on the service provider side and a reduction in the cognitive load on the user. In conventional protocols such as BIP 70, it was possible to dynamically generate a payment request, including the remittance amount and expiration date in addition to the destination address, for each transaction. This has the advantage of preventing not only address tampering but also amount tampering simultaneously. However, realizing this flexibility necessitates the maintenance and management of a secure server by the service provider to dynamically create and distribute payment data, which leads to increased management costs and an expanded attack surface.

In contrast, this method limits the target of information to semi-static data: the binding of a destination address and a domain name. As a result, not only is the dynamic server management load on service providers mitigated, but the CA is also freed from issuing signatures on a per-transaction basis, which makes it possible to reduce the overall operational burden.

## 6.2 Evaluation Against Attacks

The proposed method provides multi-layered defense, performing verification by both the system and the human, against address tampering caused by Man-in-the-Middle attacks on the communication path and Man-in-the-Mobile attacks within the device.

First, the integrity of the data is cryptographically guaranteed by verifying the digital signature using the CA's public key. Consequently, even if the destination address is altered slightly, the fraudulent request is immediately rejected due to a signature mismatch. Second, there are attacks where an attacker presents signed data for a different domain obtained through legitimate processes. In this case, since the consistency of the data itself is maintained, the signature verification on the system will succeed. However, in this system, after passing the verification, the domain name is confirmed on the cold wallet's screen, enabling verification with human-readable strings instead of a complex hexadecimal address display. As a result, the user can notice that the destination differs from the intended one during the visual confirmation stage and manually reject the transaction.

## 6.3 Consideration on Utilizing a Certificate Revocation List (CRL)

In this system, if a fraudulent signature were to be issued, there is an issue that the cold wallet alone cannot invalidate the signature until the expiration date (*expires*) passes. As a mitigation measure for this issue, utilizing a Certificate Revocation List (CRL) can be considered. However, since the cold wallet assumes an offline environment physically isolated from external networks, the device itself cannot actively retrieve the latest CRL. Instead, it relies on periodic data transfers via an online device, resulting in a time lag that depends on the transfer frequency. Although it lacks complete real-time capability, this mechanism can be considered practical. According to the empirical study by Zhang et al. [14], it has been confirmed that 95% of CAs sign and issue a new CRL within 24 h. Because revocation information is updated at such a high frequency, establishing an operational procedure to periodically transfer the latest CRL via an online device serves as a realistic countermeasure against the time lag.

### 6.4 Limitations

The following three points are cited as limitations of this system.

The first limitation is the impact of internal time deviation in the cold wallet (offline) environment on the verification of the signature's expiration date. Although it is unlikely that the device's internal clock will deviate significantly, in an offline environment where time synchronization via a network is not performed, the possibility of a certain degree of error occurring in the verification of the signature's expiration date cannot be denied.

The second limitation is that, despite systematic verification and the use of human-readable domain names, the system ultimately relies on the user to visually confirm and approve the destination on the screen.

The third limitation is the risk of service provider private key compromise. If the private key is compromised, an attacker could request a valid signature from the CA using the legitimate domain and a malicious address, leading to an unauthorized update of the smart contract and the subsequent fraudulent redirection of users' payments to the attacker's address.

## 7 Conclusion

In this study, we proposed a method to prevent the tampering of destination addresses that occurs when an online device is compromised by malware or other threats during crypto asset transactions using a cold wallet.

Conventional cold wallet operations rely on users' visual confirmation to verify the validity of an address, which is a complex sequence of alphanumeric characters, making them vulnerable to attacks such as substitution with similar addresses. In contrast, this method applied the concept of the existing BIP 70 Payment Protocol to smart contracts, eliminating the need for a payment request generation server on the service provider side, which was conventionally required. By adopting an architecture that registers the signature for the binding of a destination address and a domain name on a smart contract in advance, the service provider is freed from the burden of dynamic server management, and the cold wallet side can verify the validity of the data retrieved from the smart contract.

In the implementation and evaluation, we constructed prototypes of the cold wallet and online device using Android devices. Through experiments using the

Sepolia testnet, we confirmed that the QR code communication and address resolution processing operate within a practical range. We demonstrated that a transaction is safely issued even when routed through an untrusted online device, owing to a multi-layered defense where the user visually confirms the domain name and authorizes the signature after successful systematic verification.

A future challenge is to implement countermeasures against the concentration of trust in the CA as a single point of failure, such as exploring the integration of multi-CA threshold signatures or decentralized identity (DID) systems while preserving its serverless nature.

**Acknowledgments.** This work was supported by JSPS KAKENHI Grant Number JP25H01106.

## References

1. Andresen, G., Hearn, M.: BIP 70: payment protocol, July 2013. https://github.com/bitcoin/bips/blob/master/bip-0070.mediawiki. Bitcoin Improvement Proposal
2. Arapinis, M., Gkaniatsou, A., Karakostas, D., Kiayias, A.: A formal treatment of hardware wallets. In: Goldberg, I., Moore, T. (eds.) Financial Cryptography and Data Security, pp. 426–445. Springer International Publishing, Cham (2019)
3. Ateniese, G., Faonio, A., Magri, B., de Medeiros, B.: Certified bitcoins. In: Boureanu, I., Owesarski, P., Vaudenay, S. (eds.) Applied Cryptography and Network Security, pp. 80–96. Springer International Publishing, Cham (2014)
4. Beedham, M.: This cryptocurrency stealing malware was blocked more than 360,000 times over the past year (2019). https://thenextweb.com/news/cryptocurrency-malware-blocked-360000-times. Acccessed 20 Oct 2025
5. Čekerevac, Z., Cekerevac, P., Prigoda, L., Al-Naima, F.: Security risks from the modern man-in-the-middle attacks. MEST J. **13**(1), 34–51 (2025)
6. Erinle, Y., Kethepalli, Y., Feng, Y., Xu, J.: SoK: design, vulnerabilities, and security measures of cryptocurrency wallets. Comput. Netw. **273**(111691), 111691 (2025)
7. Garba, A., Guan, Z., Li, A., Chen, Z.: Analysis of man-in-the-middle of attack on bitcoin address. In: Proceedings of the 15th International Joint Conference on e-Business and Telecommunications, pp. 388–395. SCITEPRESS - Science and Technology Publications (2018)
8. Ivanov, N., Yan, Q.: EthClipper: a clipboard meddling attack on hardware wallets with address verification evasion. In: 2021 IEEE Conference on Communications and Network Security (CNS), pp. 191–199 (2021). https://doi.org/10.1109/CNS53000.2021.9705033
9. Khan, A.G., Zahid, A.H., Hussain, M., Riaz, U.: Security of cryptocurrency using hardware wallet and QR code. In: 2019 International Conference on Innovative Computing (ICIC), pp. 1–10 (2019). https://doi.org/10.1109/ICIC48496.2019.8966739
10. Tiwari, S.: An introduction to QR code technology. In: 2016 International Conference on Information Technology (ICIT), pp. 39–44 (2016). https://doi.org/10.1109/ICIT.2016.021

11. Tsuchiya, T., Dong, J.D., Soska, K., Christin, N.: Blockchain address poisoning (2025). https://arxiv.org/abs/2501.16681
12. Wright, C.S.: Bitcoin: a peer-to-peer electronic cash system. SSRN Electron. J. (2008). https://doi.org/10.2139/ssrn.3440802
13. Zaghloul, E., Li, T., Mutka, M.W., Ren, J.: Bitcoin and blockchain: security and privacy. IEEE Internet Things J. **7**(10), 10288–10313 (2020)
14. Zhang, L., et al.: Analysis of SSL certificate reissues and revocations in the wake of Heartbleed. In: Proceedings of the 2014 Conference on Internet Measurement Conference (2014). https://api.semanticscholar.org/CorpusID:1720946
15. Zhou, Y., Jiang, X.: Dissecting android malware: characterization and evolution. In: 2012 IEEE Symposium on Security and Privacy. IEEE, May 2012

# Public-Blockchain-Based Federated Learning with Fully On-Chain Aggregation

Taichi Matsumoto(✉), Taisei Takahashi, and Kazumasa Omote

University of Tsukuba, Tsukuba, Japan
{s2520560,takahashi.taisei.fw}@u.tsukuba.ac.jp, omote@risk.tsukuba.ac.jp

**Abstract.** Federated learning has attracted attention as a privacy-preserving machine learning method, but its reliance on an aggregation server creates a single point of failure and limits transparency in the aggregation process. Although blockchain has been proposed as a solution, most existing studies either only record model update histories and evaluation results or rely on consortium blockchains or proprietary platforms, which do not provide objective trustworthiness through public verification. To address these issues, this study proposes a federated learning system with fully on-chain aggregation on a public blockchain. By executing model aggregation through smart contracts, the proposed method removes trust dependence on a specific administrative entity for the aggregation process and enables public verification of its correctness. To mitigate information leakage on a public ledger, we integrate differential privacy. To cope with computational resource constraints on public blockchains, we also introduce a segmented aggregation protocol that processes model parameters in segments. We evaluated the proposed method on Optimism Sepolia, a Layer 2 blockchain. The results show that the proposed method maintains model performance comparable to that of standard federated learning, enables on-chain aggregation under gas constraints through the segmented aggregation protocol, and retains utility under differential privacy. Evaluation of gas cost and execution time further indicates the practical feasibility of the proposed method in a Layer 2 environment.

**Keywords:** Blockchain · Public blockchain · Federated learning · On-chain aggregation · Smart contracts · Differential privacy

## 1 Introduction

In recent years, the demand for machine learning using large-scale data has rapidly increased across many fields. In particular, in domains such as healthcare and finance, learning across multiple organizations is required to build highly accurate models. However, in these domains, data cannot easily be shared externally because of personal data protection regulations such as the GDPR and


H. Huang et al. (Eds.): ICBC 2026, LNCS 16959, pp. 17–32, 2027.
https://doi.org/10.1007/978-3-032-36766-2_2

conflicting interests among organizations, and aggregating data in a single location remains challenging.

Federated learning (FL) has attracted attention as a solution to these challenges. Federated learning is a distributed machine learning method that emphasizes privacy protection. Each participant trains a model using its own local data and shares only model updates for aggregation to construct a global model. In this way, collaborative machine learning across multiple organizations becomes possible without sharing raw data externally.

However, conventional federated learning generally relies on a single aggregation server. This creates a trust dependency on a specific administrative entity and leads to limited transparency, a single point of failure, and centralization.

Blockchain has the potential to mitigate this problem by providing a decentralized and publicly verifiable execution platform. However, most existing studies use blockchain only to record model updates and evaluation results, while the aggregation itself remains off-chain. As a result, the correctness of the aggregation computation cannot be fully verified, and the trust dependency on the aggregation process is not fundamentally removed. Although some studies perform aggregation on-chain, most of them assume consortium blockchains. Because consortium blockchains are operated by a predefined set of organizations, they cannot structurally eliminate participant exclusivity or the risk of collusion among operating entities.

Therefore, a public blockchain is a more suitable basis for objective verification of model aggregation. To the best of our knowledge, however, no prior study has experimentally evaluated a federated learning system that directly executes model aggregation on a public blockchain. Moreover, once model updates are handled on a public ledger, ensuring confidentiality also becomes an important challenge.

To address these issues, this study proposes a federated learning system with fully on-chain aggregation on a public blockchain. The proposed method executes model aggregation through smart contracts, thereby eliminating trust dependence on a specific administrative entity for the aggregation process and enabling public verification of the computation. To cope with gas-limit constraints, we introduce a segmented aggregation protocol that processes model parameters in segments. To mitigate information leakage on a public ledger, we also integrate differential privacy. Furthermore, we evaluate the proposed method on Optimism, a Layer 2 blockchain, in terms of model performance, gas cost, and execution time.

Using the MNIST and UCI Adult datasets, we show that the proposed method maintains model performance comparable to that of conventional federated learning while demonstrating the feasibility of on-chain aggregation on a public blockchain.

The main contributions of this study are as follows.

- **Proposal of a federated learning system with fully on-chain aggregation on a public blockchain:** We propose a system that executes model aggregation solely through smart contracts on a public blockchain, eliminating trust dependence on a specific administrative entity and enabling public verification of the correctness of the computation process.

- **Proposal of a segmented aggregation protocol for gas constraints:** We design a segmented aggregation protocol that enables on-chain aggregation under gas constraints even when the number of model parameters or participants increases.
- **Integration of differential privacy for confidentiality protection:** We integrate differential privacy and evaluate whether confidentiality can be achieved while maintaining practical model performance on a public ledger.
- **Practicality evaluation using a Layer 2 blockchain:** Through experiments on Optimism, we evaluate the gas cost and execution time of on-chain aggregation and show its practicality in a Layer 2 environment.

# 2 Preliminaries

## 2.1 Blockchain

A blockchain (BC) is a distributed ledger technology in which each node on a P2P network maintains the same ledger. Each block is linked in chronological order by hash values, thereby providing tamper resistance and high fault tolerance. Smart contracts running on this infrastructure are programs that autonomously execute processing according to predefined conditions. They enable transparent execution of transactions and contracts without relying on a third party. Ethereum is a representative platform that employs smart contracts [3,13].

In recent years, Layer 2 blockchains (L2BCs) have been used to mitigate the scalability and fee issues of Ethereum. Optimism [8], which is used in this study, is a rollup-based L2BC that executes the main part of transaction processing on Layer 2 while posting the data to Ethereum. It therefore provides a lower-cost and higher-throughput execution environment than Ethereum while preserving the transparency, public verifiability, and independence from a specific administrative entity of the underlying public blockchain.

**Gas and Block Gas Limit.** On smart contract platforms such as Ethereum and Optimism, executing computation and recording data require a fee called gas. Gas quantifies the consumption of network resources and protects the system from infinite loops and malicious attacks. Each block has an upper limit on the total amount of gas it can contain, called the block gas limit. If a single transaction exceeds this limit, it cannot be executed and results in an out-of-gas failure. Therefore, in the design of systems on public blockchains, this constraint on physical computational resources is a major obstacle.

## 2.2 Federated Learning

Federated learning (FL) is a distributed learning method in which each client trains a model using only local data without sharing raw data externally. In each round, the current global model is distributed to the clients, each client performs local training, and only the resulting model updates are transmitted and aggregated to produce a new global model.

**Application in This Study: Federated Averaging (FedAvg).** This study adopts Federated Averaging (FedAvg) [6], a standard federated learning algorithm. In FedAvg, the global model is updated by computing a weighted average of the locally trained models according to the number of samples held by each client.

### 2.3 Differential Privacy

Differential privacy (DP), proposed by Dwork et al. [5], is a framework for preventing the identification of a specific individual's data from the output of an algorithm by adding noise. In this study, we use the Gaussian mechanism, which is suitable for high-dimensional model parameters, and adopt Local DP (LDP), in which each client adds noise locally before transmission. This is because, in a public blockchain environment, Central DP is not suitable from the viewpoint of confidentiality protection, as raw local models before aggregation would be visible on the ledger. The aim is to achieve client-level DP and reduce leakage of information about a specific client's data characteristics through the model.

## 3 Related Work

### 3.1 Blockchain for Management and Integrity

Many studies use blockchain mainly for logging, access control, or incentives rather than as a direct aggregation platform. FedBlockHealth [11] and FlwrBC [4] use blockchain to record model updates and manage incentives, but aggregation itself remains off-chain. RRAFL [15] also limits blockchain to storing management information, without addressing the transparency or correctness of model aggregation itself. Zhou et al. [17] proposed a federated blockchain-enabled architecture for 6G streaming, highlighting the use of blockchain-based trust mechanisms in distributed service environments.

### 3.2 Off-Chain Aggregation with Integrity Assurance

Some studies use external storage together with blockchain to reduce on-chain storage and computation costs. FedBlocks [9] uses IPFS and blockchain to support aggregation integrity, but the actual aggregation process still depends on a centralized component. Zhao et al. [16] delegate aggregation to a specific participant, but this still requires trust in the aggregation entity and is not experimentally validated on an operational blockchain platform.

### 3.3 On-Chain Aggregation

On-chain aggregation is the closest direction to our approach. However, BAFFLE [10] reduces gas cost by training only part of the model, which limits learning performance and convergence. DeepChain [12] adopts a consortium blockchain and therefore does not provide the openness or public verifiability of a public blockchain. A recent IIoT-oriented method [14] also relies on a proprietary execution environment and has not been evaluated on existing public blockchain platforms such as Ethereum or Optimism. In addition, it does not provide concrete consideration of privacy protection.

### 3.4 Position of This Study

Most prior studies use blockchain only for recording, incentive management, or integrity support, while aggregation remains off-chain and dependent on specific entities [4,9,11,15–17]. Thus, they do not make the aggregation computation publicly verifiable. Even on-chain aggregation studies often rely on consortium blockchains or proprietary platforms, limiting openness and public verifiability [10,12,14].

In contrast, this study executes aggregation through smart contracts on an existing public Layer 2 blockchain, removing trust dependence on a specific aggregation entity and enabling public verification. It also addresses gas constraints with a segmented aggregation protocol and mitigates information leakage by integrating differential privacy.

**Fig. 1.** System overview

## 4 Proposed Method

### 4.1 System Overview

This study proposes a federated learning system that executes model aggregation on a public blockchain to eliminate dependence on a centralized aggregation server in conventional federated learning.

The assumed use case is collaborative training by multiple organizations that keep their confidential data locally and cannot fully trust either other participants or a specific administrative entity.

As shown in Fig. 1, the proposed method replaces the centralized aggregation server with a smart contract. In this way, the aggregation process is executed on the blockchain and its correctness can be verified by an unspecified number of participants. While this eliminates trust dependence on the aggregation server, the reliability of updates from individual participants remains an important issue, which is discussed in Sect. 6.

This architecture provides the following properties.

- **Transparency and trustworthiness:** Because the aggregation logic is published and fixed on the ledger, malicious tampering by a server operator is technically prevented.
- **Elimination of a single point of failure:** Because the system does not depend on a centralized server, it avoids failure caused by server outage or external attack.

### 4.2 Approximate Gas Cost Equations and Definition of Physical Constraints

To operate the proposed method in a real environment, the gas consumed by a single transaction must remain below the block gas limit $G_{limit}$ in the following two phases.

**Constraint in Parameter Transmission.** The estimated gas consumption $G_{sub}$ when each client writes local model parameters to the smart contract is expressed as follows.

$$G_{sub} \approx G_{base} + (L \times G_{store}) \tag{1}$$

Here, $G_{base}$ is the base transaction cost, $L$ is the number of parameters per segment, and $G_{store}$ is the storage cost per element. In practice, the physical constraint $G_{sub} < G_{limit}$ must be satisfied.

**Constraint in On-Chain Aggregation.** The estimated gas consumption $G_{agg}$ when the smart contract aggregates the parameters from all clients is expressed as follows.

$$G_{agg} \approx G_{base} + (K \times L \times G_{calc}) + (L \times G_{update}) \tag{2}$$

Here, $K$ is the number of clients, $G_{calc}$ is the unit cost of weighted-average computation, and $G_{update}$ is the cost of updating the global model. Because the computational load depends on the product of the number of clients $K$ and the number of parameters $L$, the physical constraint $G_{agg} < G_{limit}$ must be satisfied.

### 4.3 System Flow

Under the physical constraints defined above, the proposed method operates as follows.

1. **Contract deployment:** The issuer deploys a smart contract that defines the total number of model parameters $D$ and the number of parameters per segment $L$ satisfying the constraint equations in Sect. 4.2.
2. **Local training:** Each participant obtains the latest global model and performs training using local data.
3. **Application of differential privacy (masking):** After training, Gaussian noise is added to the parameters to ensure Local Differential Privacy (LDP).
4. **Parameter transmission:** Each client divides the parameters into segments of length $L$ and sends them in multiple transactions so that the constraint in Sect. 4.2 is satisfied.
5. **On-chain aggregation:** The smart contract executes aggregation according to the constraints in Sect. 4.2, depending on the number of clients $K$ and the number of parameters $L$. If batch processing is not possible, aggregation proceeds incrementally according to the segmented aggregation protocol described in the next subsection.

### 4.4 Segmented Aggregation Protocol

The segmented aggregation protocol is a method that divides the parameters to be aggregated into appropriate sizes according to the total number of model parameters $D$ and the number of participating clients $K$. This enables aggregation of large-scale models while avoiding blockchain write constraints such as gas limits.

- **Segmentation with respect to the number of parameters** $D$: If $D$ is large and the transmission cost $G_{sub}$ for a single client exceeds the limit, the parameters are segmented so that transmission can be completed.
- **Segmentation with respect to the number of clients** $K$: Even when $D$ is small, if $K$ is large, the aggregation cost $G_{agg}$ may exceed the limit. In this case, the contract restricts the range to be aggregated at one time and distributes the process across multiple transactions, thereby avoiding execution failure due to transaction rejection.

## 5 Experimental Evaluation

This section presents the experimental settings and results used to evaluate the proposed method on Optimism Sepolia. We evaluate model performance, execution time, gas cost, and the effect of differential privacy through two experiments: comparison with conventional methods on MNIST and UCI Adult without differential privacy, and evaluation of model performance and privacy protection on UCI Adult with differential privacy.

### 5.1 Experimental Settings

**Experimental Environment**

- **Blockchain**: Optimism Sepolia
- **Languages and frameworks**: Python 3.10, PyTorch, Solidity 0.8.0, Web3.py
- **On-chain aggregation**: FedAvg implemented in Solidity
- **Integer scaling**: model parameters were converted to integers with a scaling factor of $10^6$ before transmission

**Rationale for Dataset Selection.** We obtained both datasets from OpenML [2] and used two datasets with different characteristics.

- **MNIST**: We used OpenML data_id = 554. In this study, it was treated as an even/odd binary classification task rather than a multi-class classification task. The input consists of $28 \times 28$ grayscale images, and the flattened input dimension is 784. The total number of parameters in the logistic regression model is 785. Because of its relatively high dimensionality in the context of on-chain processing, this dataset is suitable for evaluating the increase in gas cost during on-chain aggregation and the necessity of the segmented aggregation protocol.
- **UCI Adult** [1]: We used OpenML data_id = 1590. This is a binary classification task for predicting whether annual income exceeds 50K from attributes such as age and occupation. It is a tabular dataset containing both numerical and categorical features. After one-hot encoding, the input dimension is 105, and the total number of parameters is 106. Because it contains personal attributes, this dataset is suitable for evaluating the trade-off between confidentiality and model performance when differential privacy is applied (Table 1).

**Table 1.** Experimental parameters for each dataset and the DP setting

| Item | MNIST | UCI Adult | UCI Adult (with DP) |
|---|---|---|---|
| Model architecture | Logistic Regression | | |
| Total number of parameters ($D$) | 785 | 106 | 106 |
| Number of clients ($K$) | 10 | 10 | 50 |
| Learning rate ($\eta$) | 0.01 | 0.01 | 0.05 |
| Batch size | 64 | 64 | 32 |
| Local epochs ($E$) | 2 | 2 | 10 |
| Total rounds ($T$) | 20 | 20 | 10 |
| Noise multiplier ($\sigma$) | - | - | 1.0 |
| Clipping norm ($C$) | - | - | 1.5 |

**Hyperparameter Settings.** In this study, we used a binary logistic regression model for all datasets, binary cross-entropy as the loss function, and SGD as the optimizer. Although large-scale models are common in federated learning, we adopted this manageable scale as an initial step to clearly evaluate gas consumption and validate the segmented aggregation protocol under the strict constraints of a public blockchain.

**Preprocessing.** For each dataset, we first split the data into training and evaluation sets to prevent data leakage. The transformations required for preprocessing were then determined from the training data and applied to the evaluation data.

- **MNIST**: Pixel values were normalized to $[0, 1]$, and each image was flattened into a 784-dimensional vector. Because the model in this study is a binary logistic regression model, labels were converted into a binary classification task in which even digits were labeled as 1 and odd digits as 0.
- **UCI Adult**: For numerical features, missing values were imputed with the median and then standardized. For categorical features, missing values were imputed with the most frequent value and then one-hot encoding was applied. Labels were set to 1 for income >50K and 0 otherwise.

In the experiment applying differential privacy to UCI Adult, Local Differential Privacy was assumed, and each participant added noise to the model updates before transmission. To control the sensitivity of the updates, an L2 norm constraint based on the specified clipping norm $C$ was applied.

For data partitioning, we adopted stratified IID partitioning that preserves class ratios, prioritizing the evaluation of the effectiveness of the on-chain aggregation platform. Although handling non-IID environments is important in practical deployment, this study first evaluates the feasibility of aggregation on a public blockchain and the preservation of model performance under IID settings.

### 5.2 Evaluation of Model Performance

We compare the proposed method with two baselines: Centralized Learning, which trains a model using all training data, and Standard FL, which executes FedAvg off-chain.

At each round, Best F1 denotes the maximum F1 score over all decision thresholds on the evaluation set.

Figures 2 and 3 compare the model performance of the proposed method, Standard FL, and Centralized Learning on MNIST and UCI Adult, respectively. On both datasets, the proposed method achieved Accuracy, AUPRC, and F1 score almost identical to those of Standard FL, although both remained below Centralized Learning. These results validate that the proposed on-chain implementation reproduces the behavior of conventional off-chain FedAvg, despite blockchain-specific constraints such as integer scaling, segmented transmission, and gas-limited execution.

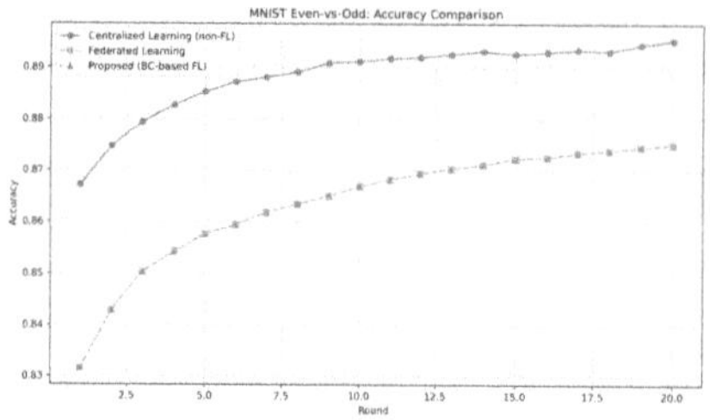


(a) Accuracy trends

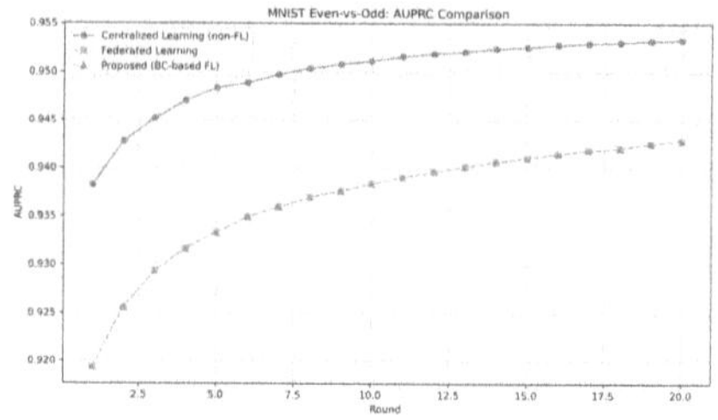


(b) AUPRC trends

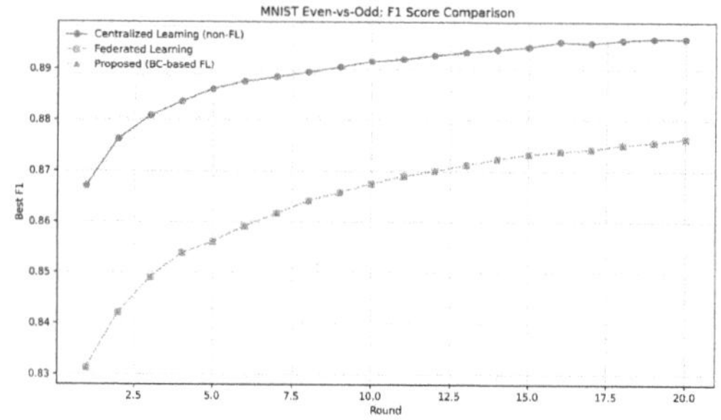


(c) Best F1 trends

**Fig. 2.** Comparison of model performance metrics on the MNIST dataset

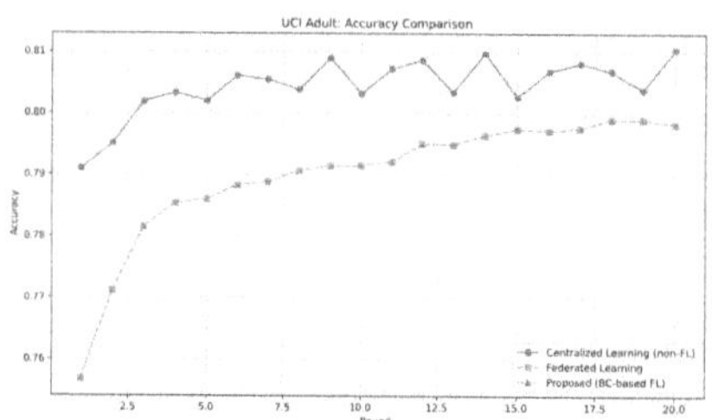


(a) Accuracy trends

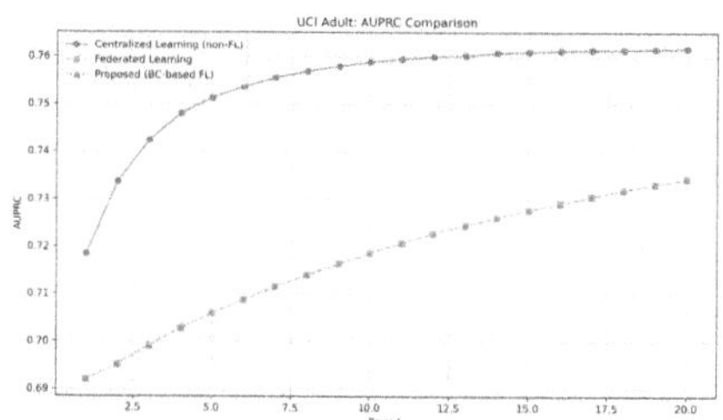


(b) AUPRC trends

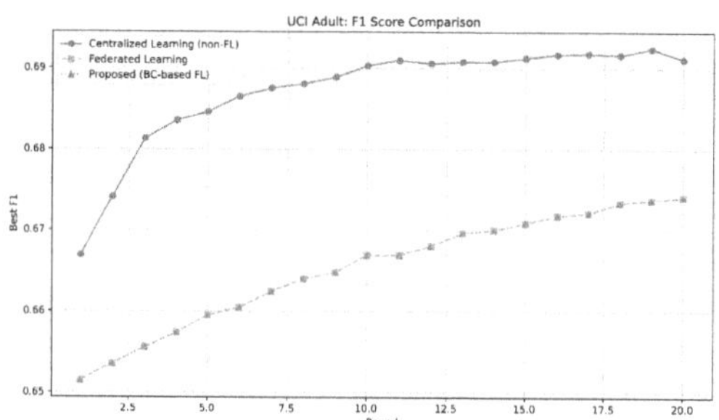


(c) Best F1 trends

**Fig. 3.** Comparison of model performance metrics on the UCI Adult dataset

**Table 2.** Average resource consumption and execution time for each dataset (2026/5/10)

| Dataset | Gas cost in Round 1 [Gas] | Average gas cost after Round 2 [Gas] | Transmission time [s] | Aggregation time [s] |
|---|---|---|---|---|
| MNIST (D = 785) | 204,433,757 (0.477 USD) | 79,981,187 (0.186 USD) | 6.71 | 6.28 |
| UCI Adult (D = 106) | 31,369,302 (0.0731 USD) | 11,815,728 (0.0275 USD) | 2.77 | 2.78 |

**Evaluation of Resource Consumption and Scalability.** This subsection evaluates the proposed method in terms of operating cost and execution time on Optimism Sepolia.

*Avoiding Physical Constraints by the Segmented Aggregation Protocol.* For MNIST, which has the largest model size ($D = 785$), transmitting all parameters at once violates the constraint $G_{sub} < G_{limit}$ for the estimated gas consumption $G_{sub}$ in Sect. 4.2 and Eq. 1, causing the transaction to fail. Therefore, we applied segmentation with respect to the number of model parameters $D$ and adjusted the number of parameters per segment $L$, so that transmission and recording were performed through multiple transactions satisfying the constraint in Eq. 1. This confirmed that even in a Layer 2 environment such as Optimism Sepolia, large-scale model processing can be completed on-chain under physical constraints.

*Analysis and Predictability of Gas Cost.* As shown in Table 2, the gas cost was much higher in Round 1 than after Round 2 for both datasets. This is because the initial storage write cost on EVM-based blockchains is higher than the cost of updating an existing value.

As shown in Table 2, MNIST ($D = 785$) required much higher gas cost than UCI Adult ($D = 106$), confirming a strong dependence of gas consumption on the number of model parameters $D$. This supports the validity of the approximate gas cost equations presented in Sect. 4.2 even in the real environment of Optimism Sepolia. Therefore, developers can estimate future operating cost from the model size and gas price.

In addition, in a rollup-based Layer 2 such as Optimism, an additional cost is required to post transaction data to Ethereum L1, in addition to the execution gas on L2. In this paper, we refer to this additional cost as the L1 data fee. Using the GasPriceOracle on Optimism Mainnet, we estimated that the total L1 data fee per round was $7.80 \times 10^{-7}$ ETH (approximately 0.00182 USD) for UCI Adult ($K = 10, D = 106$) and $3.00 \times 10^{-6}$ ETH (approximately 0.00698 USD) for MNIST ($K = 10, D = 785$). These results confirm that the L1 data fee increases with model size and the number of segmented transactions. However, its share of the total cost was still small, about 1.1% for MNIST and 1.8% for UCI Adult, indicating that under our experimental conditions the main cost still comes from execution gas on L2.

*Execution Time and Scalability.* We measured the average transmission time per client and the time required for on-chain aggregation after receiving all data. The results are shown in Table 2. Note that these execution times may vary depending on external factors such as each client's network connection and overall blockchain congestion.

For high-dimensional models, the communication and computation overhead increases because transactions must be issued sequentially for each segmented block of parameters, and each transaction must wait for inclusion in a block and finalization. As shown in Table 2, both transmission and aggregation took longer for MNIST than for UCI Adult. This indicates that the increase in the number of transactions caused by higher-dimensional models also affects execution time. Nevertheless, on-chain aggregation completed on the order of seconds for both datasets, suggesting that the segmented aggregation protocol combined with a Layer 2 execution environment is practical under gas constraints.

### 5.3 Evaluation of the Impact of Differential Privacy

This subsection evaluates model performance and the privacy budget ($\epsilon$) when Local Differential Privacy is applied to the UCI Adult dataset. The cumulative $\epsilon$ is computed using the Rényi Differential Privacy [7] accountant. We denote the proposed method with differential privacy as DP-BC-FL and that without differential privacy as BC-FL without DP. We conducted five runs with different random seeds and report the mean and standard deviation at each round. To mitigate the effect of noise, we increased the number of local epochs to 10 and the number of clients to 50.

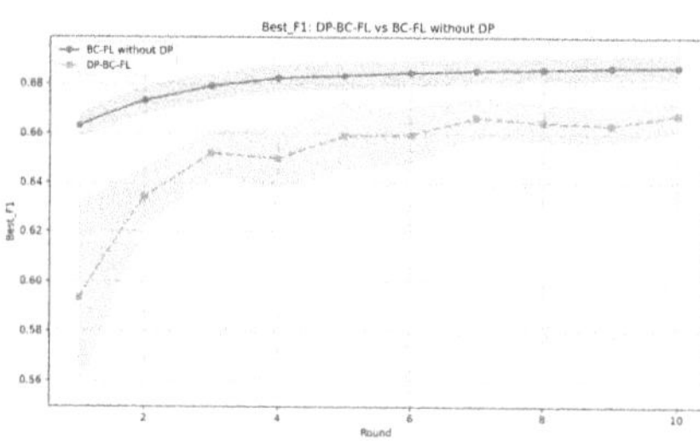


**Fig. 4.** Comparison of Best F1 on UCI Adult with and without differential privacy

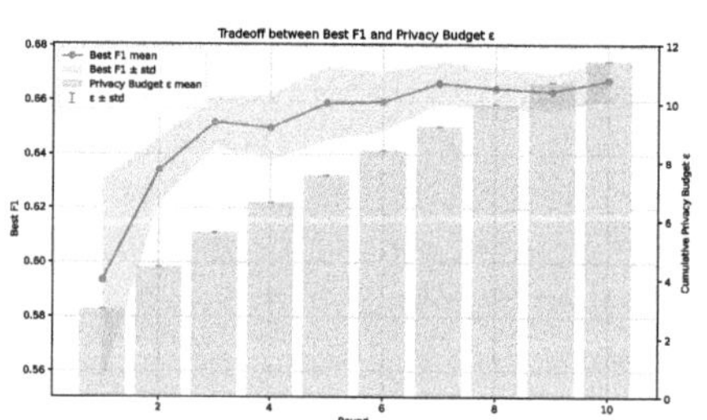


**Fig. 5.** Cumulative $\epsilon$ and Best F1 on UCI Adult

**Performance Trends and Privacy Consumption.** Figure 4 shows that, although DP-BC-FL achieved lower Best F1 than BC-FL without DP, its performance continued to improve as the rounds progressed, indicating that the proposed method retains utility under differential privacy. The variance of DP-BC-FL was also larger in the early rounds and became smaller as learning progressed.

Figure 5 shows that cumulative $\epsilon$ increased monotonically and exceeded approximately 11 in the final round, while the improvement in Best F1 saturated after the middle rounds. This suggests that early stopping around the saturation point can avoid additional privacy loss with little utility gain.

It should also be noted that an acceptable privacy budget depends on the application context and threat assumptions. Therefore, the observed $\epsilon$ characterizes the privacy–utility trade-off under the evaluated setting and does not establish a universal criterion for practical deployment.

**Table 3.** Resource consumption for UCI Adult with differential privacy (2026/5/10)

| Gas cost in Round 1 [Gas] | Average gas cost after Round 2 [Gas] | Transmission time [s] | Aggregation time [s] |
|---|---|---|---|
| 149,906,030 | 55,788,137 | 2.93 | 3.46 |
| (0.35 USD) | (0.13 USD) | | |

**Need for the Segmented Aggregation Protocol with More Clients.** To mitigate the effect of noise and improve the signal-to-noise ratio during aggregation, we increased the number of clients from 10 to 50. As indicated by Sect. 4.2 and Eq. 2, this increases the aggregation cost $G_{agg}$. As shown in Table 3, the differential privacy setting required substantially higher gas cost than the UCI Adult setting without differential privacy ($K = 10$), while transmission and aggregation still completed on the order of seconds.

Thus, applying differential privacy increases the aggregation load through the larger number of clients. We addressed this issue by segmenting with respect to the number of clients $K$, limiting the range processed at one time by the smart contract and performing aggregation incrementally. This confirms that the segmented aggregation protocol supports both privacy-oriented client scaling and on-chain aggregation.

# 6 Discussion

## 6.1 On-Chain Aggregation vs. Verifiable Off-Chain Aggregation

Off-chain aggregation schemes can reduce on-chain computation by using external verification mechanisms such as zero-knowledge proofs (ZKPs) or trusted execution environments (TEEs). ZKP-based schemes require proof generation and verification, while TEE-based schemes rely on trusted hardware and attestation. Because aggregation is executed outside the blockchain, these approaches introduce additional verification assumptions, implementation complexity, and processing delays caused by proof generation, attestation, and data transmission.

In contrast, the proposed method performs aggregation directly through the blockchain execution engine. Therefore, it does not depend on external verification mechanisms, and the correctness of the aggregation computation is enforced by the smart contract and the blockchain protocol. In addition, because the computation result is finalized when the block is recorded, no additional proof-generation or attestation phase is required. Although this comes with a trade-off in gas cost, the ability to complete the entire process, from aggregation execution to result finalization, consistently within the blockchain is an effective design for federated learning, where consistency is important.

### 6.2 Trust Issues on the Participant Side, Contribution Evaluation, and Incentive Design

This study focuses on the trust problem in the model aggregation process that has conventionally been handled by a centralized aggregation server in federated learning. The proposed method makes at least the operations handled by the aggregation server verifiable without depending on the honesty of a specific administrative entity.

On the other hand, this study does not guarantee the integrity of the model updates sent by individual participants. In other words, directly preventing poisoning attacks by malicious participants or low-quality updates is outside the scope of this study. Therefore, what this study resolves is trust dependence on the aggregator, while the problem of participant honesty remains as future work.

To address this issue, possible approaches include contribution evaluation, robust aggregation, anomaly detection, and reputation-based weighting. For example, approximate Shapley Value computation could be used to quantify the impact of each client's update on model performance, while robust aggregation or anomaly detection could help identify malicious or low-quality updates. These mechanisms could filter or down-weight inappropriate updates and improve convergence and trustworthiness even in the presence of malicious participants.

Furthermore, in the proposed method, each participant must pay transaction fees when sending model updates to the blockchain. This is an operational challenge specific to the use of a public blockchain, but it may be mitigated by linking contribution evaluation to incentive design. Specifically, a possible approach is to distribute rewards according to each participant's contribution and offset the gas cost incurred during transmission. Therefore, introducing contribution evaluation is important from both the perspective of preventing malicious updates and that of economic sustainability.

## 7 Conclusion

This study proposed a federated learning system with fully on-chain aggregation on a public blockchain and evaluated its feasibility on Optimism Sepolia. The results showed that the proposed method eliminates trust dependence on a centralized aggregation server, maintains model performance comparable to standard federated learning, and remains feasible under gas constraints through the segmented aggregation protocol. They also showed that differential privacy can be integrated while retaining utility and that a Layer 2 blockchain makes the proposed method practical in terms of gas cost and execution time.

Future work includes evaluating convergence in non-IID settings and implementing a contribution evaluation system to assess participant updates, filter malicious or low-quality updates, and support incentive design.

**Acknowledgments.** This work was supported by JSPS KAKENHI Grant Numbers JP26K21213 and JP25H01106.

## References

1. Becker, B., Kohavi, R.: Adult. UCI Machine Learning Repository (1996)
2. Bischl, B., et al.: OpenML: insights from 10 years and more than a thousand papers. Patterns **6**(7), 101317 (2025). https://www.cell.com/patterns/fulltext/S2666-3899(25)00165-5
3. Buterin, V., et al.: Ethereum white paper. GitHub Repository **1**, 22–23 (2013)
4. Cam, N.T., Kiet, V.T.: FlwrBC: incentive mechanism design for federated learning by using blockchain. IEEE Access **11**, 107855–107866 (2023)
5. Dwork, C.: Differential privacy. In: Bugliesi, M., Preneel, B., Sassone, V., Wegener, I. (eds.) Automata, Languages and Programming, pp. 1–12. Springer, Heidelberg (2006)
6. McMahan, B., Moore, E., Ramage, D., Hampson, S., Arcas, B.A.Y.: Communication-efficient learning of deep networks from decentralized data. In: Singh, A., Zhu, J. (eds.) Proceedings of the 20th International Conference on Artificial Intelligence and Statistics, vol. 54, pp. 1273–1282. PMLR (2017)
7. Mironov, I.: Rényi differential privacy. In: IEEE 30th Computer Security Foundations Symposium (CSF), pp. 263–275. IEEE (2017)
8. Optimism Foundation: Optimism. https://www.optimism.io/. Accessed 7 May 2026
9. Purohit, R.M., Verma, J.P., Jain, R., Kumar, A.: FedBlocks: federated learning and blockchainbased privacy-preserved pioneering framework for IoT healthcare using IPFS in web 3.0 era. Clust. Comput. **28**(2), 139 (2025)
10. Ramanan, P., Nakayama, K.: BAFFLE: blockchain based aggregator free federated learning. In: 2020 IEEE International Conference on Blockchain (Blockchain), pp. 72–81 (2020)
11. Waheed, N., et al.: FedBlockHealth: a synergistic approach to privacy and security in IoT-enabled healthcare through federated learning and blockchain. In: GLOBECOM 2023 - 2023 IEEE Global Communications Conference, pp. 3855–3860 (2023)

12. Weng, J., Weng, J., Zhang, J., Li, M., Zhang, Y., Luo, W.: DeepChain: auditable and privacy-preserving deep learning with blockchain-based incentive. IEEE Trans. Dependable Secure Comput. **18**(5), 2438–2455 (2021)
13. Wood, G., et al.: Ethereum: a secure decentralised generalised transaction ledger. Ethereum Project Yellow Paper **151**(2014), 1–32 (2014)
14. Yang, Q.: Blockchain-based decentralized federated learning with on-chain model aggregation and incentive mechanism for industrial iot. IEEE Open J. Commun. Soc. **5**, 6420–6429 (2024)
15. Zhang, J., Wu, Y., Pan, R.: Incentive mechanism for horizontal federated learning based on reputation and reverse auction. In: Proceedings of the Web Conference 2021, pp. 947–956 (2021). Association for Computing Machinery (2021)
16. Zhao, Y., et al.: Privacy-preserving blockchain-based federated learning for IoT devices. IEEE Internet Things J. **8**(3), 1817–1829 (2021)
17. Zhou, Z., Wei, K., Song, T.: A federated blockchain-enabled 6g streaming architecture: protocol innovation and trusted ecology. In: Shyamasundar, R.K., Huang, H., He, S., Fang, J., Zhang, L.J. (eds.) Blockchain - ICBC 2025, pp. 117–133. Springer Nature Switzerland, Cham (2026)

# An AI Smart Contract System with Incentivized Off-Chain Training and On-Chain Model Evaluation

Yuta Yoshida(✉) and Kazumasa Omote

University of Tsukuba, Tsukuba, Ibaraki, Japan
s2620574@u.tsukuba.ac.jp

**Abstract.** Implementing AI models on smart contracts enables autonomous AI services whose processing logic and results can be verified by third parties. However, because smart contracts incur gas costs according to computational complexity, executing computationally intensive processes such as training on-chain is impractical. For this reason, existing studies have mainly adopted architectures in which only inference is performed on-chain, while training and evaluation are delegated to off-chain environments. In such architectures, however, it is difficult to verify and reject submitted models on-chain when they exhibit insufficient performance or fail to satisfy predefined evaluation conditions.

In this paper, we propose a method that delegates the training process to external off-chain servers in a competition-based manner, while executing model evaluation within a smart contract. In the proposed method, submitted model parameters are evaluated on-chain based on acceptance conditions specified by the Owner, and only models satisfying these conditions are adopted. This enables the smart contract to manage the consistency between the model used for evaluation and the model used in actual operation without trusting the off-chain servers. In addition, the proposed design includes an incentive mechanism that can reward the submitter of the selected model and allows the model to be continuously updated on the same contract.

To demonstrate the feasibility of the proposed method, we implemented a system consisting of smart contracts and off-chain servers, and measured the transaction costs associated with on-chain evaluation and related processes for three types of multilayer perceptrons. The prototype focuses on model submission, on-chain evaluation, activation, inference, and access control, while monetary processes such as fee deposits and reward transfers are left as design components.

**Keywords:** AI Smart Contract · On-Chain Model Evaluation · Incentive Mechanism


H. Huang et al. (Eds.): ICBC 2026, LNCS 16959, pp. 33–48, 2027.
https://doi.org/10.1007/978-3-032-36766-2_3

# 1 Introduction

## 1.1 Background

Blockchain is a decentralized ledger that is extremely difficult to tamper with. Smart contracts running on blockchains are programs that automatically execute processes according to predefined conditions, enabling high transparency and reliability without requiring a central administrator. Owing to these characteristics, smart contracts have been increasingly applied in various domains, such as finance, supply chain management, and voting systems [1,2].

On the other hand, conventional AI services face several challenges. For example, it is not easy to guarantee the trustworthiness of model developers or to verify whether a model has been replaced with an inappropriate one during operation. When AI is used from smart contracts such as decentralized applications (DApps), a common architecture is to call off-chain AI services through APIs, which inevitably requires trust in the external services. In addition, developing and operating machine learning models require specialized knowledge and sufficient computational resources. Therefore, it is difficult for users without sufficient expertise or computational resources to safely develop and operate such models.

By incorporating AI models into smart contracts, model structures and parameters can be recorded in a tamper-resistant manner, allowing third parties to verify their contents and execution results. For example, when used as decision-making modules for access control or workflow automation, AI models can automate processes such as access permission, additional authentication, approval, payment, and escalation to human review based on scores computed from input features. Furthermore, if machine learning models can be solicited in a competition-based manner with rewards, even users without sufficient expertise or computational resources can outsource model development and operate the obtained models on smart contracts.

However, smart contracts have inherent constraints: gas costs increase with the computational complexity of contract execution and storage operations [3, 4], making it impractical to execute computationally intensive processes on-chain. Furthermore, in Ethereum and many Ethereum Virtual Machine (EVM)-compatible blockchains, EIP-170 limits the deployable contract bytecode size to 24 KB, or 24,576 bytes [5]. Under such gas and code-size constraints, it is difficult to implement the entire machine learning pipeline, including training, evaluation, and inference, fully on-chain. Therefore, existing studies that directly implement machine learning models on smart contracts have mainly adopted approaches in which training and evaluation are performed off-chain, while only inference is executed on-chain. However, in such approaches, even if models with insufficient performance or models that do not satisfy predefined evaluation conditions are submitted, it is difficult to verify and reject them on-chain.

Regarding the verification of machine learning models, several studies have proposed using zero-knowledge proofs to verify that confidential models correctly execute inference and training processes according to prescribed procedures [6–

8]. These methods are useful because they can prove the correctness of computation results without revealing model parameters. However, as the model size increases, the time and computational cost required for proof generation also increase.

Based on this background, this study proposes a smart contract system that evaluates models submitted by external off-chain servers on a blockchain and adopts only models that satisfy predefined acceptance conditions. In the proposed system, computationally intensive training processes are delegated to external off-chain servers in a competition-based manner. However, because the evaluation of submitted models is executed within the smart contract based on criteria specified by the Owner, there is no need to trust the off-chain servers. In addition, the proposed design can provide incentives to the submitter of the selected model, thereby encouraging competitive model submissions from multiple off-chain servers. This realizes a mechanism for adopting and operating only models that satisfy the evaluation conditions on-chain, without trusting the correctness of off-chain model submitters.

### 1.2 Related Work

Several studies have implemented machine learning models on smart contracts and performed on-chain inference. Kadadha et al. implemented a trained decision tree model on a smart contract for task allocation in crowdsourcing [9]. Li et al. proposed ML2SC, which converts MLPs constructed in PyTorch into Solidity and enables transparent and tamper-resistant inference on the EVM using PRBMath-based fixed-point arithmetic [10,11]. These studies improve transparency by executing inference on-chain, but they mainly focus on using trained models and do not sufficiently address on-chain verification of whether submitted models satisfy predefined acceptance conditions.

Other studies have investigated the evaluation and selection of machine learning models on smart contracts. Kurtulmuş et al. proposed an incentive-based mechanism that delegates model development, evaluates submitted models on-chain, and determines the best model [12]. Rana et al. proposed a transparent evaluation and selection mechanism for multiple machine learning models in Android malware detection [13]. In addition, some studies execute model inference and performance calculation off-chain and record evaluation results or rankings on a blockchain [14,15]. These studies enhance the transparency of model evaluation and selection, but they do not mainly focus on continuously operating the selected model on a smart contract or ensuring on-chain consistency between the model used during evaluation and the model used during actual operation.

There are also studies that verify the correctness or improve the trustworthiness of machine learning models using methods other than blockchain. For example, zkCNN verifies the correctness of confidential CNN inference using zero-knowledge proofs [7], and zkDL verifies the training process of deep learning models [8]. These methods can verify computation without revealing model parameters, but their proof-generation cost increases as models become more complex. Other studies address malicious behavior detection [16–18] and model provenance management [19,20]; however, they focus on different aspects from this study, such as behavioral soundness and provenance tracking.

Finally, several studies have delegated part of the processing to external environments to compensate for blockchain limitations, such as off-chain signature generation for smart contracts [21] and computation delegation to Trusted Execution Environments [22,23]. These studies are related to this work in that they complement the limitations of on-chain processing by using external environments. In contrast, this study manages the evaluation, adoption, operation, and updating of submitted models in an integrated manner on smart contracts, while delegating only the training process to external servers.

### 1.3 Contributions

This study proposes an AI smart contract system that evaluates models submitted by off-chain servers on-chain and adopts only models satisfying predefined acceptance conditions. Its main contributions are as follows.

- We realize a mechanism that evaluates machine learning models within a smart contract and automatically adopts only models that satisfy the acceptance conditions specified by the model owner. This prevents models with insufficient performance or models that do not satisfy the evaluation conditions from being adopted on-chain, thereby enabling quality control based on observable evaluation metrics. The evaluation results can also be checked on the smart contract before the model is used.
- We design a workflow that manages the process from evaluation to operation in an integrated manner within a smart contract. By allowing only the model used for evaluation to be operated, the proposed system ensures consistency between the evaluated model and the model used in actual operation. Furthermore, even when model performance degrades, the model can be updated without redeployment by submitting new model parameters to the same smart contract.
- We introduce an incentive mechanism as a design component for delegating model training to external off-chain servers. In the proposed method, incentives can be sent to the submitter of the selected model only when the evaluation result satisfies the specified conditions. This encourages participation and competition among multiple servers, enabling model owners without specialized knowledge or sufficient computational resources to outsource model development by preparing data and rewards.

## 2 Proposed System

This section describes the proposed method for operating machine learning models within smart contracts. The proposed method delegates computationally intensive training to off-chain servers, while executing model evaluation and post-adoption inference on-chain. This enables submitted models to be adopted and operated only when they satisfy the owner's acceptance conditions. Figure 1 illustrates the overview of the proposed system and the data and control flows among the Owner, off-chain Servers, Users, and the three contracts. Submitted model parameters are evaluated by the Model Evaluation Contract, and the Model Management Contract activates only models satisfying the acceptance condition $\tau$. After activation, Users obtain inference results through the Model Inference Contract.

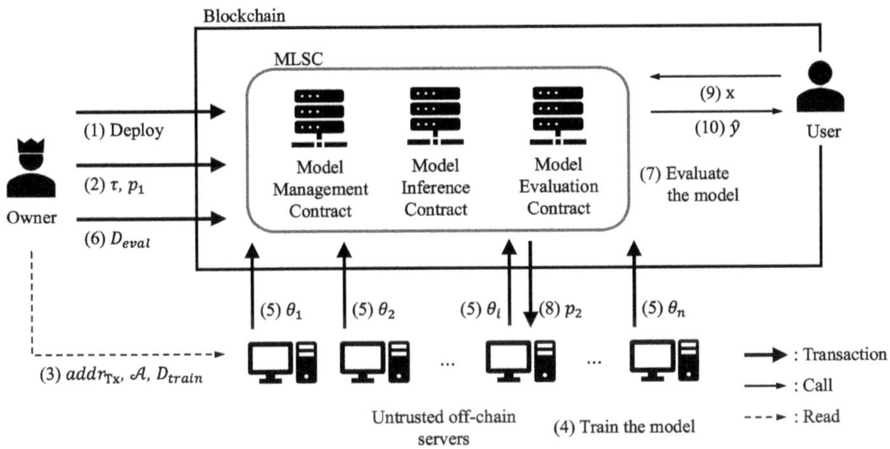


**Fig. 1.** Overview of the proposed system

## 2.1 Challenges to Be Addressed

Executing and operating machine learning models on smart contracts involves five main challenges: high gas costs for training and evaluation, on-chain verification of whether submitted models satisfy the owner's acceptance conditions, trustless acceptance or rejection of off-chain trained models, separation of privileges among entities such as the Owner, Server, and User, and the 24 KB bytecode size limitation imposed by EIP-170 [5]. To address these challenges, the proposed method delegates training off-chain while determining model evaluation, adoption, and operation on-chain.

## 2.2 Notation

The notation used in the proposed method is shown in Table 1.

## 2.3 Entities

This section describes the four entities involved in the proposed system.

**Table 1.** Notation

| Symbol | Description |
|---|---|
| MLSC | Smart contract for model operation |
| $addr_{\mathrm{M}}$ | Wallet address of the Model Management Contract |
| $addr_{\mathrm{I}}$ | Wallet address of the Model Inference Contract |
| $addr_{\mathrm{E}}$ | Wallet address of the Model Evaluation Contract |
| $\tau$ | Acceptance condition for the evaluation result $\mathbf{s}$ |
| $p_1$ | Cryptocurrency deposited by the Owner for model training delegation |
| $p_2$ | Cryptocurrency sent as an incentive for model training |
| $\mathcal{A}$ | Model architecture, such as the number of layers, the number of nodes in each layer, and activation functions |
| $D_{train}$ | Training dataset |
| $D_{eval}$ | Evaluation dataset |
| $\theta$ | Model parameters after training |
| $\mathbf{x}$ | Feature vector, i.e., input |
| $\hat{p}$ | Predicted probability output by the model |
| $\hat{y}$ | Predicted label |
| $\mathbf{s}$ | Evaluation metric vector representing the evaluation result |

- The Owner is the entity that constructs and manages the system. The Owner deploys the MLSC, manages Owner privileges, sets the acceptance conditions, registers the evaluation dataset, and sets the fee for delegating model training. The Owner also publishes the training dataset, model architecture, and the addresses of the contracts constituting the MLSC to off-chain servers, thereby delegating model training.
- The off-chain Server is an external entity responsible for training machine learning models. The Server trains a model based on the training dataset and model architecture published by the Owner, and sends the obtained model parameters to the Model Inference Contract. In the proposed method, the Server is not assumed to always behave honestly; therefore, whether a submitted model is accepted or rejected is determined based on on-chain evaluation.
- The MLSC is a set of smart contracts that operate the proposed system. It consists of three contracts: the Model Management Contract, the Model Inference Contract, and the Model Evaluation Contract. The Model Management Contract is the central contract responsible for controlling the overall system, including evaluation requests, management of evaluation results, activation of models that satisfy the acceptance conditions, and incentive transfers in the proposed design. The Model Inference Contract receives model parameters from off-chain servers, stores the submitted model parameters, and executes inference using the activated model. The Model Evaluation Contract calculates the evaluation result $\mathbf{s}$ of the submitted model based on the evaluation dataset and determines whether it satisfies the predefined acceptance condition $\tau$.
- The User is the entity that sends a feature vector $\mathbf{x}$ to the Model Inference Contract and obtains inference results from the activated model. This operation can be executed only after a model has been activated.

### 2.4 Access Control

In the proposed method, access control is introduced to securely manage operations on smart contracts. Each contract manages the privileges granted to Owners on an address-by-address basis and verifies the caller's address when executing operations that require authorization. The Owner can grant and revoke Owner privileges, set the incentive amount, set the acceptance condition $\tau$, register the evaluation dataset, and permanently stop model updates. On the other hand, operations such as viewing evaluation results and executing inference using an activated model are made publicly available, thereby ensuring transparency and usability when the model is used.

### 2.5 Attack Model

In this study, we assume that the Owner, the blockchain, and the smart contracts are trusted. In contrast, external off-chain servers responsible for model training are not necessarily assumed to behave honestly, and may exhibit malicious behavior. The purpose of the proposed method is to evaluate models submitted by such off-chain servers on-chain and adopt only models that satisfy predefined acceptance conditions. However, this study does not address tampering with or intentional leakage of the evaluation dataset by the Owner, nor does it aim to completely detect backdoor behaviors that do not appear in the evaluation dataset.

Based on these assumptions, we consider the following attack models.

- Submission of inappropriate parameters: A malicious off-chain server intentionally generates a low-performance model or inappropriate model parameters whose degradation is observable through the evaluation metrics, and submits them to the smart contract.
- Parameter replacement during operation: A malicious off-chain server attempts to make the system use model parameters that have not passed evaluation as the operational model.
- System disruption: An off-chain server intentionally submits a large number of inappropriate model parameters to the MLSC, thereby disrupting the evaluation process or model update operations.

### 2.6 Overview of MLSC Processing

This section describes the processing overview of the three contracts that constitute the MLSC. In the proposed method, the functions of model management, inference, and evaluation are not integrated into a single contract, but are separated into the Model Management Contract, Model Inference Contract, and Model Evaluation Contract. This clarifies the responsibility of each process and addresses the contract size limitation in the EVM.

**Model Management Contract.** The Model Management Contract is the central contract responsible for managing the state of the entire MLSC. This contract requests the Model Evaluation Contract to perform evaluation and records the returned evaluation result $\mathbf{s}$. If the evaluation result $\mathbf{s}$ satisfies the predefined acceptance condition $\tau$, the corresponding model is managed as a candidate model. The acceptance condition $\tau$ defines the minimum requirement for candidate models, whereas the ranking criterion determines the best model among them. When multiple models satisfy $\tau$, the best model is selected and activated based on a metric or a combination of metrics specified in advance by the Owner. In addition, in the proposed design, the incentive $p_2$ can be sent to the off-chain Server that submitted the best model.

**Model Inference Contract.** The Model Inference Contract is responsible for storing model parameters and executing inference. Off-chain servers submit the parameters $\theta$ of trained models to the Model Inference Contract. This contract stores the submitted model parameters and calculates the predicted probability $\hat{p}$ and predicted label $\hat{y}$ for an input feature vector $\mathbf{x}$ during both evaluation and use. However, users can perform inference only with models that have been activated by the Model Management Contract.

**Model Evaluation Contract.** The Model Evaluation Contract is responsible for evaluating the performance of submitted models. Using the evaluation dataset $D_{eval}$ registered by the Owner, this contract obtains inference results from the model stored in the Model Inference Contract and calculates the evaluation result $\mathbf{s}$. It then determines whether the calculated evaluation result $\mathbf{s}$ satisfies the acceptance condition $\tau$ set by the Owner and returns the result to the Model Management Contract. This enables the acceptance or rejection of models submitted by off-chain servers to be determined on-chain, without directly trusting the submitted models.

### 2.7 Procedure

Based on Fig. 1 and Fig. 2, the procedure of the proposed method is described below.

(1) The Owner deploys the contracts that constitute the MLSC on the blockchain: the Model Management Contract, the Model Inference Contract, and the Model Evaluation Contract.
(2) The Owner registers the acceptance condition $\tau$ in the Model Management Contract and deposits cryptocurrency to be used as an incentive for model training delegation.
(3) The Owner publishes the addresses of the contracts constituting the MLSC, the model architecture $\mathcal{A}$, and the training dataset $D_{train}$ for off-chain servers.
(4) The off-chain servers obtain the published training dataset $D_{train}$ and model architecture $\mathcal{A}$, and train models.

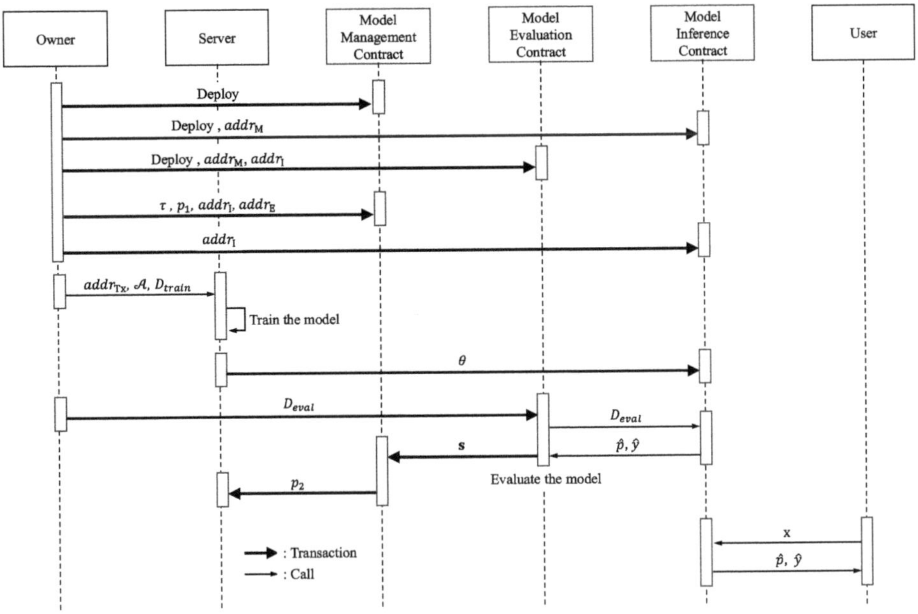


**Fig. 2.** Sequence diagram of the proposed system

(5) The off-chain servers send the parameters $\theta$ of the trained models to the Model Inference Contract. The Model Inference Contract records the submitted model parameters and the submitter addresses.
(6) After the submission period ends, the submitted parameters are fixed for the update round, and later modifications or additional submissions are excluded from the evaluation target of that round. The Owner then registers the evaluation dataset $D_{eval}$ in the Model Evaluation Contract.
(7) The Model Evaluation Contract performs inference on $D_{eval}$ using the submitted model parameters, calculates the evaluation result $\mathbf{s}$ from $\hat{p}$ and $\hat{y}$, and returns it to the Model Management Contract.
(8) The Model Management Contract selects and activates the best model among those satisfying $\tau$. In the proposed design, it can also send an incentive to the selected model submitter.
(9) The User sends a feature vector $\mathbf{x}$ to the Model Inference Contract.
(10) The Model Inference Contract executes inference using the activated model parameters, and the User obtains the inference result.

If model performance degrades during operation, steps (2)–(8) can be repeated on the same smart contracts to update the model without redeployment.

# 3 Implementation Evaluation

To confirm that the proposed method can function practically, we implemented a prototype of the entire system consisting of smart contracts and off-chain servers. In this implementation, we focused on the main functions of the proposed system, including the submission of model parameters from off-chain servers to smart contracts, on-chain model evaluation, inference using activated models, and access control, excluding monetary processes related to the model training delegation fee and incentive transfers. In the evaluation, we verify that these main operations function correctly and measure the transaction costs required for each process to examine whether the proposed method remains feasible under practical operating conditions. Thus, this evaluation focuses on the feasibility and transaction cost of the on-chain workflow rather than on comparing the predictive performance of specific models.

## 3.1 Environment

The implementation was conducted on Apothem, the test network of XDC Network, which is an EVM-compatible blockchain. The smart contracts were implemented in Solidity based on the MLP model code presented by Li et al., and the PRBMath library was used for fixed-point arithmetic [10,11]. Li et al. report that the on-chain implementation using PRBMath-based fixed-point arithmetic produces inference outputs and classification performance identical to those of the off-chain PyTorch implementation. Following this implementation approach, our prototype executed inference and evaluation using fixed-point arithmetic within smart contracts.

In this implementation, we used multilayer perceptrons (MLPs) as the target models for on-chain evaluation and inference because their structure is relatively simple and suitable for smart contract implementation. As shown in Table 2, we used three types of MLPs with two hidden layers and different numbers of neurons. ReLU was used in the hidden layers, and Sigmoid was used in the output layer. For Model C, the Model Inference Contract was split by computation stage: the first contract computes the first layer and ReLU activation, and the second contract executes the remaining layers using the 16-dimensional fixed-point intermediate vector returned by the first contract. The gas overhead of this inter-contract call is included in the measured cost for Model C.

**Table 2.** List of implemented models

| Model name | Number of hidden layers | Number of neurons |
|---|---|---|
| Model A | 2 layers | 17–4–4–1 |
| Model B | 2 layers | 17–8–8–1 |
| Model C | 2 layers | 17–16–8–1 |

In this implementation, Accuracy, Brier score, Precision, Recall, and F1 score were calculated on-chain as model evaluation metrics. These metrics enable us to examine the overall classification performance, the validity of predicted probabilities, and the tendencies of false positives and false negatives in positive-class detection. As the dataset, we used Soladoye's dataset for an epilepsy onset prediction task [24], which contains 17 features and binary class labels. A Windows PC was used as the off-chain server, and the executed transactions were confirmed through a blockchain explorer compatible with XDC Apothem.

### 3.2 Experimental Procedure

We connected to the XDC Apothem testnet and deployed the smart contracts constituting the proposed method on the blockchain. Then, while interacting with a Windows PC regarded as an off-chain server, we uploaded model parameters, registered the evaluation dataset, executed on-chain evaluation, and performed inference from another smart contract. We measured the transaction cost required for each process. The processes evaluated in the experiment are as follows.

(1) Deployment of the Model Management Contract
(2) Deployment of the Model Inference Contract
(3) Deployment of the Model Evaluation Contract
(4) Registration of the Model Inference Contract
(5) Registration of the Model Evaluation Contract
(6) Registration of the Owner
(7) Setting of the acceptance condition $\tau$
(8) Upload of one set of bias parameters
(9) Upload of one set of weight parameters
(10) Upload of the evaluation dataset
(11) Execution of evaluation, including model activation
(12) Execution of inference from another smart contract

### 3.3 Results

Table 3 shows the transaction costs required for each process in this experiment. The values in the table are rounded to the fifth decimal place.

The total transaction costs required for the entire workflow of the proposed method were 0.46717, 0.66353, and 1.04130 TXDC for Model A, Model B, and Model C, respectively. Assuming that 1 XDC was equivalent to 0.0330 USD as of May 14, 2026, these costs correspond to approximately 0.0154 USD, 0.0219 USD, and 0.0344 USD, respectively. Although Apothem is a test network and the USD conversions are therefore only reference values, the results suggest that the proposed method could be operated at a practical cost on low-cost EVM-compatible blockchains.

**Table 3.** Transaction costs required for each process (TXDC)

| Process | Model A | Model B | Model C |
|---|---|---|---|
| (1) Deployment of the Model Management Contract | 0.04326 | 0.04326 | 0.04326 |
| (2) Deployment of the Model Inference Contract | 0.06631 | 0.06655 | 0.10388 |
| (3) Deployment of the Model Evaluation Contract | 0.03971 | 0.03971 | 0.03971 |
| (4) Registration of the Model Inference Contract | 0.00061 | 0.00061 | 0.00061 |
| (5) Registration of the Model Evaluation Contract | 0.00064 | 0.00064 | 0.00064 |
| (6) Registration of the Owner | 0.00034 | 0.00034 | 0.00034 |
| (7) Setting of the acceptance condition $\tau$ | 0.00082 | 0.00082 | 0.00082 |
| (8) Upload of one set of bias parameters | 0.00341 | 0.00594 | 0.00905 |
| (9) Upload of one set of weight parameters | 0.03110 | 0.06955 | 0.13192 |
| (10) Upload of the evaluation dataset | 0.12002 | 0.12049 | 0.12352 |
| (11) Execution of evaluation, including model activation | 0.15263 | 0.29775 | 0.55460 |
| (12) Execution of inference from another smart contract | 0.00833 | 0.01743 | 0.03296 |
| Total | 0.46717 | 0.66353 | 1.04130 |

# 4 Discussion

## 4.1 Security

This section discusses the security of the proposed method, mainly assuming the submission of inappropriate models by off-chain servers. In the proposed method, model parameters submitted by off-chain servers are not adopted directly. Instead, the Model Evaluation Contract calculates the evaluation result $\mathbf{s}$, and the Model Management Contract determines whether the result satisfies the acceptance condition $\tau$. Therefore, even if a model with insufficient performance or an inappropriate model whose degradation is observable through the evaluation metrics is submitted, it is not activated as the operational model unless it satisfies the acceptance condition. In addition, during model updates, newly submitted model parameters are not adopted unless they pass on-chain evaluation, thereby preventing unevaluated models from being operated. Furthermore, because the availability of model updates is managed by the Owner, a third party cannot arbitrarily replace the operational model. However, since the evaluation dataset $D_{eval}$ is registered on a public blockchain, it becomes observable by external parties after registration. Therefore, in the proposed system, model submissions are closed and the submitted parameters are fixed before $D_{eval}$ is registered in each update round. In addition, if the same $D_{eval}$ is reused across multiple rounds, future submitters may submit models overfitted to the previously disclosed evaluation data. Thus, in practical operation, it is necessary to register a different evaluation dataset for each update round.

An off-chain Server may also submit many inappropriate model parameters to disrupt evaluation or model updates, increasing the Owner's burden and transaction costs. However, parameter submission itself incurs transaction costs, so continuous disruption requires the attacker to bear such costs. Moreover, because incentives can be paid only to the Server that submits the best-performing model, the proposed method economically encourages legitimate submissions rather than long-term disruption. Nevertheless, submitted model parameters are observable on the blockchain, which may allow front-running through copied resubmissions. This issue can be mitigated by combining the proposed method with a commit-reveal scheme, in which a Server first registers a commitment based on the model parameters and a random nonce, and later reveals the actual parameters for verification.

This study assumes that the Owner, the blockchain, and the smart contracts are trusted; therefore, cases in which the Owner itself is involved in malicious behavior are outside the scope of this work. For example, if the Owner prepares inappropriate training or evaluation data, such misconduct cannot be detected by the proposed method alone. In addition, if an attacker impersonates the Owner and publishes malicious training data, off-chain servers may train models using that data, resulting in the submission of many inappropriate models. To address this issue, the validity of the training data can be verified by registering the hash value of the training dataset in the MLSC in advance and allowing off-chain servers to compare it with the hash value of the downloaded training dataset.

### 4.2 Efficiency and Scope of Application

It is important to keep transaction costs within a practical range, especially for uploading evaluation data and repeatedly performing inference on it, whose costs increase with data and model size. Using Apothem as an example of a low-cost EVM-compatible blockchain, we confirmed that the workflow, including evaluation and updates, can be executed at a practical cost. Since model updates do not require redeployment, additional costs are mainly limited to parameter upload, evaluation, and activation.

In this implementation, we implemented on-chain evaluation and inference for small-scale MLP models. In EVM-compatible blockchains, EIP-170 limits the bytecode size that can be uploaded in a single deployment to approximately 24 KB. Therefore, it is difficult to deploy a model with a large amount of code or a large number of parameters as a single contract. This limitation can be partially mitigated by splitting the contract into multiple contracts; in fact, for Model C, we divided the Model Inference Contract into two contracts and confirmed that evaluation and inference could be executed. However, contract splitting is an implementation-level technique for mitigating the bytecode size limitation, and does not demonstrate applicability to large-scale models in general.

Thus, the proposed method is suitable for lightweight models with limited inference complexity, such as MLPs with a relatively small number of layers and neurons, rather than large-scale AI services targeting many general users. For models with many parameters or models whose computational complexity increases with the input size, evaluation dataset size, or sequence length, transaction costs for evaluation and inference may become excessive, even if the bytecode size limitation is mitigated by contract splitting. Since XDC Network is an EVM-compatible chain, the smart contracts and system architecture used in this implementation can also be ported to other low-cost EVM-compatible chains.

### 4.3 Use Cases and Limitations

The proposed method is suitable for applications where transparency, auditability, and automatic execution are more important than model confidentiality, such as access control, workflow automation, classification in DAOs and Web3 applications, and model competitions using public data. In such applications, the Owner must specify the acceptance condition $\tau$ according to the target task. If the threshold is too strict, all submitted models may be rejected, whereas if it is too loose, low-quality models may be adopted. Therefore, in practical deployments, $\tau$ should be set based on the performance of existing models or validation datasets.

Because model architectures, parameters, and on-chain evaluation datasets are publicly visible, the method is not directly suitable for applications requiring strong confidentiality, such as medical, insurance, or financial credit-scoring applications. Such cases require additional mechanisms, including zero-knowledge proofs, encryption, or off-chain evaluation.

In addition, smart contracts using the proposed method are basically assumed to be deployed on the same blockchain as the DApps that use them. Therefore, cooperation with applications on other blockchains requires additional mechanisms such as bridges or oracles.

## 5 Conclusion

In this study, we proposed an AI smart contract system that evaluates machine learning models within smart contracts and adopts only models satisfying predefined acceptance conditions. The proposed method delegates model training to off-chain Servers in an incentive-based competition, while executing evaluation and inference on-chain. This prevents low-quality models from being adopted without trusting off-chain Servers and manages the consistency between the evaluated and operational models. We implemented a prototype on Apothem, the test network of XDC Network, and confirmed that the workflow for three small-scale MLP models can be executed at a cost equivalent to less than 0.04 USD.

The proposed method assumes a trusted Owner and cannot address manipulation of evaluation data or acceptance conditions by the Owner. It also handles model architectures and parameters on-chain, making it unsuitable for applications requiring confidentiality of models or evaluation data. Furthermore, this implementation is a prototype evaluation based on small-scale MLP models, and additional validation is required to examine its generalizability to other model configurations. Future work includes improving confidentiality through zero-knowledge proofs and commitments, examining the practical limits of contract splitting for larger model architectures, extending the method to lightweight models other than MLPs, and comparing cost-security trade-offs with zero-knowledge-proof-based approaches.

**Acknowledgments.** This work was supported by JSPS KAKENHI Grant Number JP25H01106.

**Disclosure of Interests.** The authors have no competing interests to declare that are relevant to the content of this article.

## References

1. Omote, K., Ikeda, T., Kono, E., Nagai, H., Mimura, N., Kashiwabara, N.: Analysis of papers and patents in the blockchain field using e-CSTI. In: Proceedings of the 6th International Conference on Blockchain Computing and Applications (BCCA 2024), pp. 163–170. IEEE (2024)
2. Omote, K., Inoue, Y., Terada, Y., Shichijo, N., Shirai, T.: A scientometrics analysis of cybersecurity using e-CSTI. IEEE Access **12**, 40350–40367 (2024)
3. Wood, G.: Ethereum: a secure decentralised generalised transaction ledger. Technical report, Ethereum Project (2014). https://ethereum.github.io/yellowpaper/paper.pdf. Ethereum Yellow Paper
4. Ethereum Foundation: Gas and fees (2026). https://ethereum.org/en/developers/docs/gas/. Accessed 26 June 2026
5. Buterin, V.: EIP-170: Contract code size limit (2016). https://eips.ethereum.org/EIPS/eip-170. Accessed 26 June 2026
6. Peng, Z., et al.: A survey of zero-knowledge proof-based verifiable machine learning. arXiv preprint arXiv:2502.18535 (2025)
7. Liu, T., et al.: zkCNN: zero knowledge proofs for CNN predictions and accuracy. In: Proceedings of the ACM Conference on Computer and Communications Security (CCS 2021), pp. 2968–2985 (2021)
8. Sun, H., et al.: zkDL: efficient zero-knowledge proofs of deep learning training. IEEE Trans. Inf. Forensics Secur. **20**, 914–927 (2025)
9. Kadadha, M., et al.: On-chain behavior prediction machine learning model for blockchain-based crowdsourcing. Futur. Gener. Comput. Syst. **136**, 170–181 (2022)
10. Li, Z., et al.: ML2SC: deploying machine learning models as smart contracts on the blockchain. In: Proceedings of the 2024 IEEE International Conference on Blockchain and Cryptocurrency (ICBC), pp. 645–649 (2024)
11. Berg, P.R.: PRBMath. https://github.com/PaulRBerg/prb-math. Online resource
12. Kurtulmuş, A.B., Daniel, K.: Trustless machine learning contracts: evaluating and exchanging machine learning models on the ethereum blockchain. arXiv preprint arXiv:1802.10185 (2018)
13. Rana, M.S., Gudla, C., Sung, A.H.: Evaluating machine learning models on the Ethereum blockchain for android malware detection. In: Proceedings of the Intelligent Computing Conference, pp. 446–461. Springer (2019)
14. Jiang, R., Li, J., Bu, W., Shen, X.: A blockchain-based trustworthy model evaluation framework for deep learning and its application in moving object segmentation. Sensors **23**(14), 6492 (2023)

15. Yazdaninejad, H., Rajarajan, M., Krol, M.: A blockchain-enabled and transparent evaluation of ML models in the decentralised marketplace. In: Proceedings of the 2024 IEEE International Conference on Blockchain (Blockchain), pp. 458–463. IEEE (2024)
16. Wang, B., et al.: Neural cleanse: identifying and mitigating backdoor attacks in neural networks. In: Proceedings of the IEEE Symposium on Security and Privacy (SP), pp. 707–723 (2019). https://doi.org/10.1109/SP.2019.00031
17. Gao, Y., Xu, C., Wang, D., Chen, S., Ranasinghe, D.C., Nepal, S.: STRIP: a defence against trojan attacks on deep neural networks. In: Proceedings of the 35th Annual Computer Security Applications Conference (ACSAC 2019). pp. 113–125 (2019)
18. Tran, B., Li, J., Mądry, A.: Spectral signatures in backdoor attacks. In: Proceedings of the 32nd International Conference on Neural Information Processing Systems (NeurIPS 2018), pp. 8011–8021 (2018)
19. Spoczynski, M., Melara, M.S., Szyller, S.: Atlas: a framework for ML lifecycle provenance and transparency. In: Proceedings of the IEEE European Symposium on Security and Privacy Workshops (EuroS&PW), pp. 448–461 (2025). https://doi.org/10.1109/EuroSPW67616.2025.00058
20. Adeyinka, A.: Securing the AI supply chain: using blockchain for verifiable AI model provenance on government clouds. SAMRIDDHI J. Phys. Sci. Eng. Technol. **17** (2025). https://doi.org/10.18090/samriddhi.v17i01.05
21. Omote, K.: Can smart contracts generate digital signatures? In: Proceedings of the 7th International Conference on Blockchain Computing and Applications (BCCA 2025), pp. 24–30. IEEE, Dubrovnik, Croatia (2025). https://doi.org/10.1109/BCCA66705.2025.11229545
22. Cheng, R., et al.: Ekiden: A platform for confidentiality-preserving, trustworthy, and performant smart contracts. In: Proceedings of the IEEE European Symposium on Security and Privacy (EuroS&P), pp. 185–200. IEEE (2019)
23. Frassetto, T., et al.: POSE: practical off-chain smart contract execution. In: Proceedings of the Network and Distributed System Security Symposium (NDSS), pp. 1–18 (2023)
24. Soladoye, A.A.: Epilepsy onset prediction. https://www.kaggle.com/datasets/dekunle1/epilepsy-onset-prediction. kaggle dataset, online resource

# Detecting Adaptive Wash Trading Behaviors in NFT Marketplaces: A Neuro-Symbolic Approach

Shamsun Nahar Shatabdy(✉), Rabiul Islam Raihan, and Razib Hayat Khan

Independent University, Dhaka, Bangladesh
2220780@iub.edu.bd, 2220222@iub.edu.bd, rkhan@iub.edu.bd

**Abstract.** Due to the increasing popularity of non-fungible tokens (NFTs), NFT marketplaces have expanded rapidly in recent years. This explosive growth has also led to more complicated wash trading patterns. In these tactics, fraudsters make transactions through intermediary wallets and use timing patterns that look like normal human behavior. These transaction patterns make it difficult to separate fraud from real trading activity. Both traditional rule-based detection systems and standard graph neural networks (GNNs) have serious weaknesses when facing these methods. GNNs can model the network structure well, but they do not properly handle timing information. In this paper, we propose a neuro-symbolic framework that combines deterministic heuristic logic with a spatio-temporal residual graph attention network (ResidualGATv2). Our model uses continuous relative temporal encoding at the edge level so that both connection patterns and transaction timing are considered together. We also use a feature masking method to make sure the heuristic signals do not leak into the neural training process. We tested our approach on 108,588 real transactions from three major NFT collections using temporal holdout validation and achieved ROC-AUC of 0.99 and PR-AUC of 0.93. Manual forensic review of all suspicious wallets found by the model confirmed that 93.6% were real wash traders. We also found five distinct evasion patterns that rule-based systems consistently fail to detect. Our results clearly show how deterministic detection systems fail, and we hope this work provides useful insights for fraud prevention in blockchain-based digital asset markets.

**Keywords:** NFT · Wash trading · Graph attention networks · Fraud detection · Blockchain · Temporal encoding

## 1 Introduction

The concept of digital ownership has been changed by Non-fungible tokens (NFTs). NFT trading platforms have already reached multi-billion-dollar transaction volumes in a short time [1,2]. The rules and regulations could not keep up


H. Huang et al. (Eds.): ICBC 2026, LNCS 16959, pp. 49–63, 2027.
https://doi.org/10.1007/978-3-032-36766-2_4

as the growth happened much faster. This situation has created a type of market manipulation where traders make the transaction with themselves to make prices and trading volumes look higher than they actually are. This action is called wash trading which damages trust in Web3 ecosystems [1,3,4]. Some studies estimate that around 38% of observable trading volume and about 60% of traded value on major platforms shows signs of manipulation [5]. Also, some platforms give rewards based on how active a user is, which unintentionally encourages people to generate fake trading activity [1,4,6,7].

Most existing research looks at manipulation detection at a general level and does not really study how fraudsters try to avoid being detected [1,4,8,9]. Traditional rule-based methods use fixed thresholds for trading speed, volume balance, and cycle patterns. Smart mule account networks that are designed to look like real traders can easily bypass these rules. GNN-based methods can capture graph structure information, but they struggle to handle time properly. Also, when fraud transactions get mixed with many legitimate trades while averaging the data, the fraud signal becomes weak and gets lost [8,9]. The key problem is that existing systems cannot analyze multi-hop network structures and precise timing patterns at the same time. As a result, many fraudulent wallets stay undetected.

To address this problem, we propose a hybrid approach that combines heuristic pseudo-labeling with a spatio-temporal residual graph attention network (ResidualGATv2). Unlike earlier hybrid methods that put heuristic features directly into the neural model [5,8,9], our framework keeps the features used for label generation completely separate from the features used for neural training. This forces the model to find patterns that rules cannot find. We also introduce a continuous relative temporal encoding method that turns raw timestamps into edge attributes that preserve trading velocity information, which solves the time-blindness problem in standard graph convolutional networks [8,9]. Through manual forensic review by two independent reviewers, we confirmed 93.6% precision and identified five evasion patterns that explain how deterministic detectors consistently fail.

## 2 Related Works

NFT market value grew from $33 million in 2020 to more than $13 billion in 2021 [1,2], driven by digital art, collectibles, and Metaverse applications [10–12]. But the anonymous nature of blockchain also made it easy for fraud to grow [3,13,14]. Wash trading shows a very uneven distribution as the small group of user do it repeatedly. Only 27.16% of repeat offenders cause 72% of suspicious transactions [1,4]. Because of the exploiting platform reward system some individuals made over $1 million [1,3,4]. Other than washtrading there are other attacks such as rug pulls and phishing [9,15]. Researchers usually collect on-chain data from services like Etherscan or Alchemy along with marketplace logs [1,2,4,7,9] as huge collections of data are available online. Then they compare this data against known fraud address lists [2,9,11,15,16]. As there is no "Know Your Customer" process, there is no verified ground truth about which accounts or wallets are actually fraud. So most detection methods rely on heuristic pseudo-labels [1,3, 8,9,13,17]. Datasets also generally do not include off-chain behavior data [4,7, 18,19]. Also there is a serious class imbalance problem because the number of normal transactions is way more than scam transactions [8,9].

To detect wash trading many different technical approaches have been tried, including Graph Isomorphism Networks (GIN) [1,4,9,15,16,20], centrality-based feature engineering with outlier detection [3,8,9,13,16], supervised learning using XGBoost and HeteroGCN [5,8,9], unsupervised clustering like K-Means [13,17,21], and smart contract monitoring [9,11,14,18,19,22]. HeteroGCN reaches 99.4% accuracy when all features are available but without structural features like PageRank [8,9] it drops to only 50%. For rug pull detection GINs reach 75.4% accuracy [15]. Standard GCNs have the fraud signal dilution problem due to equal-weight message passing, and fixed thresholds can be bypassed by accounts that stay just below the detection limit. Most importantly, no existing work studies how sophisticated adversaries change their behavior over time to avoid detection—and that is exactly the gap we try to fill.

## 3 Proposed Framework

Our neuro-symbolic framework, illustrated in Fig. 1 uses a spatio-temporal residual graph attention network (ResidualGATv2) for NFT wash trading detection. It combines deterministic heuristic logic (Symbolic Layer) with adaptive neural learning (Neural Layer) to address two main challenges: information leakage and temporal relationship modeling.

### 3.1 Data Engineering and Feature Extraction

We collected 108,588 transaction records for 7,275 tokens from renowned blue-chip NFT collections (CryptoPunks, Bored Ape Yacht Club, and Pudgy Penguins) through the OpenSea API. This dataset contains 35,230 distinct wallet addresses.

**Graph Based Transaction Modeling:** We converted the raw transaction records into a directed graph where the seller and buyer addresses are nodes, and each transaction represents a directed edge $e = (u, v, t, a, V)$ from the seller to the buyer that contains the following information: seller address, buyer address, transaction timestamp in UNIX, unique NFT token ID, and transaction value in ETH. We extracted 35 related features for each wallet, which can be categorized into three groups (Table 1).

**Inter-transaction Time Coefficient** ($CV_{\Delta t}$): The time gaps between consecutive transactions are different between bots and human. The coefficient of variation $CV_{\Delta t} = \sigma(\Delta t)/\mu(\Delta t)$ is nearly zero for bots as they trends to trade as fixed time intervals. On the other hand, because of the irregular nature of human trading, this value is much higher. Apart from this coefficient, we also

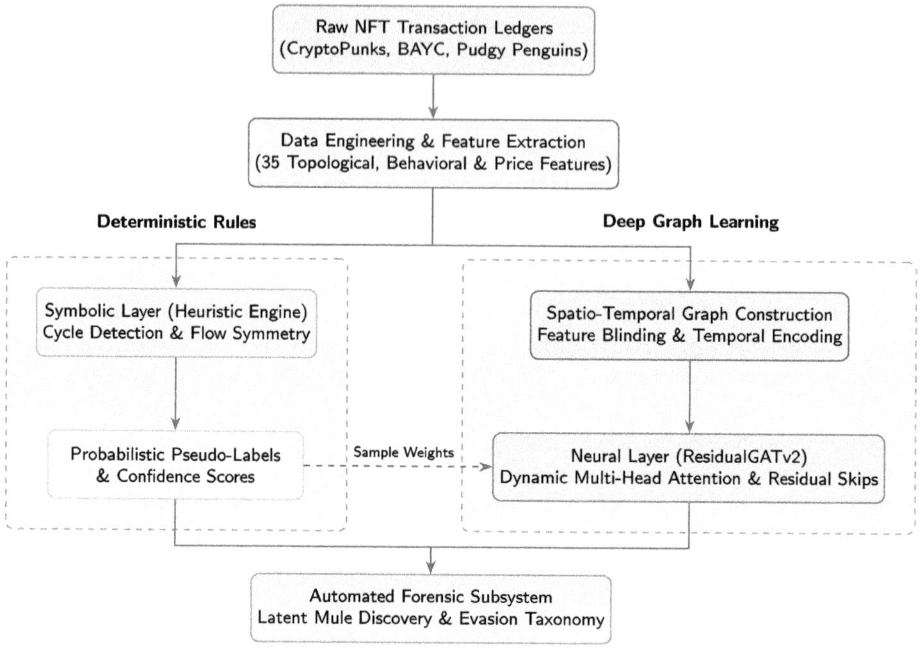


**Fig. 1.** Proposed neuro-symbolic framework for NFT wash trading detection.

**Table 1.** Engineered feature space (35 dimensions)

| Category | Features |
|---|---|
| Price-based (11) | PnL statistics (average profit margin, profit consistency/std, profitable trade ratio, zero-profit ratio), price signals (total volume, average buy price, average sell price, price coefficient of variation, round-price ratio), quick flip profitability |
| Behavioral (11) | Inter-transaction time coefficient of variation, temporal entropy (hour-of-day distribution), nocturnal activity ratio, counterparty interaction patterns (unique counterparties, repeat ratio, maximum repeat count), asset diversity (unique NFTs, concentration), speculation indicators (quick flip count, average quick flip profit), total transaction count |
| Topological (13) | Degree metrics (in-degree, out-degree, total degree, degree ratio), reciprocity, PageRank score, k-core number, ego-network properties (1-hop size and density), neighborhood degree statistics (average, maximum, standard deviation), unique neighbors |

calculated the hourly and nocturnal transaction rates, which also create a distinction between automated and human-made transactions.

**Dual-Pointer Profit and Loss State Machine:** Simple volume-based metrics are not enough to catch zero-profit wash traders. We calculate profit margins using a FIFO matching algorithm that requires $t_{Sell} > t_{Buy}$. For each matched buy-sell pair, the relative profit margin is:

$$P_k = \frac{V_S - V_B}{\max(V_B, \epsilon)} \times 100 \quad (1)$$

where $\epsilon = 10^{-4}$ ETH prevents division-by-zero issues. This gives us features like average profit, profit consistency, zero-profit ratio, and quick flip frequency.

### 3.2 Rule-Based Heuristic Annotation (Symbolic Layer)

Since there is no verified ground truth in NFT markets, our symbolic layer produces probabilistic silver labels using rule-based reasoning.

**Financial Flow Symmetry:** Wash traders usually have almost equal money going in and out. We measure this through the financial flow ratio ($F_R$):

$$F_R = \frac{|Volume_{in} - Volume_{out}|}{Volume_{in} + Volume_{out}} \quad (2)$$

Wallets with high transaction bursts ($Burst_{1h} > 30$) and near-zero balance ($F_R < 0.10$) are flagged as suspicious.

**Circular Trade Detection:** We use breadth-first search to find wallets that receive back NFTs they previously sent, within a four-hop radius.

**Probabilistic Confidence Scoring:** We convert detection signals into confidence scores ($\mathcal{C}$) used as sample weights during training. Very clear bot behavior ($Burst_{1h} > 50$ or $F_R < 0.05$) gets $\mathcal{C} = 0.95$; standard suspicious cases yield $\mathcal{C} = 0.75$; legitimate wallets receive $\mathcal{C} = 0.80$. This graduated scheme stops the neural layer from simply memorizing fixed heuristic thresholds.

### 3.3 Spatio-Temporal Graph Construction

In this section we have explained how we prepare our transaction data to build the graph.

**Temporal Data Splitting:** We sort transactions by their transaction timestamp $t$ and split into three non-overlapping sets: the first 60% for training, the next 20% for validation, and the final 20% for testing.

**Feature Isolation:** To stop the neural network from reconstructing heuristic logic by observing the features used to create labels, we remove 15 heuristic-correlated variables from the neural input: burst count features (1h, 4h, 24h windows), flow ratio ($F_R$), cycle-related topological features (in-degree, out-degree,

degree ratio, reciprocity), and behavioral threshold features (repeat ratio, max repeat count, zero-profit ratio). This forces the model to discover new discriminative patterns. All nine baseline models use the same 20-feature subset for fair comparison.

**Relative Time Encoding:** For each transaction edge $e = (u, v)$ at time $t_{u \to v}$, we calculate how long since the sender's first transaction: $\Delta t_{u \to v} = t_{u \to v} - t^{(u)}_{first}$. We then apply log-scale normalization:

$$\tilde{e}_{u \to v} = \frac{\ln(1 + \max(0, \Delta t_{u \to v}))}{\ln(1 + \Delta t^{train}_{max})} \tag{3}$$

The resulting value $\tilde{e}_{u \to v} \in [0, 1]$ encodes both structural position and trading speed as a single edge attribute, making it possible to reason jointly about graph topology and transaction timing.

### 3.4 Graph Neural Architecture and Optimization

To stop fraud signals from getting diluted during uniform neighbor aggregation, ResidualGATv2 uses dynamic multi-head attention based on the GATv2 formulation [23], extended to also include our temporal encoding $\tilde{e}_{ij}$. For each attention head $k$, the unnormalized attention score is:

$$e^{(k)}_{ij} = \mathbf{a}^{(k)\top} \text{LeakyReLU}\left(\mathbf{W}^{(k)}_1 \boldsymbol{h}_i + \mathbf{W}^{(k)}_2 \boldsymbol{h}_j + \mathbf{W}^{(k)}_e \tilde{e}_{ij}\right) \tag{4}$$

The matrix $\mathbf{W}^{(k)}_e \in \mathbb{R}^{d \times 1}$ is the only new part we add compared to standard GATv2—it projects the scalar temporal edge value into the attention computation space. Everything else follows the original GATv2 specification [9]. We prevent over-smoothing through residual skip connections and layer normalization:

$$\boldsymbol{h}^{(l+1)}_i = \text{Dropout}\Big(\text{GELU}\Big(\text{LayerNorm}\big(\boldsymbol{h}^{(l)}_i + \text{GATv2}^{(l)}\big)\Big)\Big) \tag{5}$$

The final embeddings go into an MLP classification head using GELU activations and dropout. We minimize a weighted negative log-likelihood loss that combines inverse class-frequency weights with the confidence scores ($\mathcal{C}_i$) from Sect. 3.2.

### 3.5 Automated Forensic Review Subsystem

This module finds hidden mule wallets—those that received high fraud predictions ($\hat{y}_{pred} \geq 0.80$) from the neural layer but were labeled legitimate by the heuristic layer. For each of these wallets, we extract the full transaction history and 1-hop ego-network subgraph for manual inspection.

### 3.6 Benchmark Models and Evaluation Metrics

We compare against nine baseline models organized into three groups.

**Traditional ML:** *KNN*—$k = 5$ neighbors, cosine similarity; *Random Forest*—100 estimators, balanced weights, max depth 20; *Isolation Forest*—unsupervised (contamination = 0.14); *MLP*—three layers (input→128→64→2), ReLU, dropout 0.3.

**Static GNN Baselines:** *GCN*—two-layer, uniform aggregation (hidden dim: 128); *Static GAT*—8 attention heads per layer, no temporal encoding; *HeteroGCN*—heterogeneous convolution with separate weight matrices for buyer and seller nodes.

**Temporal Baseline:** *TGN*—memory-based temporal graph learning. Under our strict inductive temporal holdout setup, TGN cannot build memory for unseen test wallets, which removes its main advantage.

**Evaluation Protocol.** All models use the same 60%–20%–20% time-based splits, the same 20-feature subset, and the same class imbalance handling through inverse-frequency weights and confidence-based sample weights. We evaluate precision, recall, F1, and ROC-AUC on the held-out test set. Each neural model is run 10 times with different seeds (42, 123, 456, 789, 1011, 1213, 1415, 1617, 1819, 1999); we report mean ± standard deviation, and use paired t-tests ($\alpha = 0.05$) to check statistical significance.

### 3.7 Manual Forensic Validation Protocol

**Sampling:** Because we do not have any verified ground truth labels to work with, we decided the best way to check if the model is actually correct was to manually go through all 141 wallets that got high-confidence fraud scores ($\hat{y}_{pred} \geq 0.80$) even though the heuristic layer said they were legitimate.

**Dual-Author Evaluation:** Both authors went through each wallet's full transaction history on their own, without knowing what the other person had decided, and also without seeing the model scores or heuristic labels. For each wallet, one of three labels was assigned: *Confirmed Wash Trader*, *Suspicious but Inconclusive*, or *Legitimate Trader*. Only wallets where both reviewers gave the same answer were kept as confirmed positives. The final agreement came out to Cohen's kappa $\kappa = 0.87$, and the four cases where we disagreed were discussed together until we reached a decision.

## 4 Experimental Results

### 4.1 Evaluation Protocol and Dataset Characteristics

Out of the 7,046 wallets, 815 were labeled as potential wash traders. Due to this high class imbalance (11.6%), we also reported the ROC-AUC and PR-AUC.

### 4.2 Classification Performance

As demonstrated by the classification performance in Table 2, our model achieves 0.97±0.00 overall accuracy, 0.99±0.00 ROC-AUC, and 0.93±0.01 PR-AUC, with recall $0.90 \pm 0.01$ and precision $0.84 \pm 0.01$ for the wash trader class. Missing a wash trader allows continued market manipulation, while excessive false positives overwhelm investigation capacity. We therefore optimize for the best balance of precision and recall, achieving the highest F1-score (0.87 ± 0.01) among all evaluated models. A false positive rate of around 16% is considered acceptable in financial fraud detection settings [5,9].

**Table 2.** Classification performance

| Class | Precision | Recall | F1-Score | Support |
|---|---|---|---|---|
| Legitimate | $0.99 \pm 0.00$ | $0.98 \pm 0.00$ | $0.98 \pm 0.00$ | 6,231 |
| Wash Trader | $0.84 \pm 0.01$ | $0.90 \pm 0.01$ | $0.87 \pm 0.01$ | 815 |
| Accuracy | $0.97 \pm 0.00$ | | | 7,046 |
| Macro Average | $0.91 \pm 0.01$ | $0.94 \pm 0.01$ | $0.93 \pm 0.01$ | 7,046 |
| Weighted Average | $0.97 \pm 0.00$ | $0.97 \pm 0.00$ | $0.97 \pm 0.00$ | 7,046 |

### 4.3 Comprehensive Baseline Comparison

Neural models were evaluated over 10 independent training runs and the comparison results are shown in the Table 3.

**Traditional Machine Learning:** While Random Forest achieved competitive performance, traditional machine learning models cannot detect multi-hop network topology. As many wash traders are distributed across interconnected wallet clusters, these models fail to detect them.

**Graph Neural Networks:** HeteroGCN [10] has the highest recall (0.97±0.01) among all baselines, but its precision is only 0.56±0.02 which gives just 71% F1. During aggregation, this model treats every neighbor the same way. As a result, many legitimate wallets get flagged as wash traders by this model. Compared to this model, our proposed model demonstrated better performance with an F1 score of($0.87 \pm 0.01$). TGN had $0.55 \pm 0.03$ precision and $0.81 \pm 0.02$ recall, which we expected. Its memory module does not really work when it has never seen the test wallets before. GCN and Static GAT both hit ROC-AUC 0.99±0.00 but their precision stays lower at 0.73 and 0.77 respectively.

**Proposed Method:** ResidualGATv2 achieves the best F1-score (0.87 ± 0.01) among all evaluated models. While HeteroGCN reaches a higher recall (0.97 ± 0.01), its precision drops to 0.56 ± 0.02, yielding an F1-score of only 0.71 ± 0.02. The proposed model maintains competitive recall (0.90 ± 0.01) while delivering a 7% point precision advantage over Static GAT. All performance gains are statistically significant ($\alpha = 0.05$).

**Table 3.** Baseline comparison.

| Category | Model | Precision | Recall | F1-Score | ROC-AUC |
|---|---|---|---|---|---|
| Traditional Machine Learning | K-Nearest Neighbors | $0.88 \pm 0.00$ | $0.75 \pm 0.00$ | $0.81 \pm 0.00$ | $0.96 \pm 0.00$ |
| | Random Forest | $0.90 \pm 0.00$ | $0.79 \pm 0.00$ | $0.84 \pm 0.00$ | $0.99 \pm 0.00$ |
| | Isolation Forest | $0.57 \pm 0.00$ | $0.50 \pm 0.00$ | $0.53 \pm 0.00$ | $0.91 \pm 0.00$ |
| | Multi-Layer Perceptron | $0.86 \pm 0.01$ | $0.81 \pm 0.02$ | $0.83 \pm 0.01$ | $0.99 \pm 0.00$ |
| Graph Neural Networks | HeteroGCN | $0.56 \pm 0.02$ | $0.97 \pm 0.01$ | $0.71 \pm 0.02$ | $0.99 \pm 0.00$ |
| | TGN | $0.55 \pm 0.03$ | $0.81 \pm 0.02$ | $0.65 \pm 0.02$ | $0.94 \pm 0.01$ |
| | GCN | $0.73 \pm 0.02$ | $0.93 \pm 0.01$ | $0.82 \pm 0.01$ | $0.99 \pm 0.00$ |
| | Static GAT | $0.77 \pm 0.01$ | $0.94 \pm 0.01$ | $0.85 \pm 0.01$ | $0.99 \pm 0.00$ |
| **Proposed** | **Spatio-Temporal ResidualGATv2** | $\mathbf{0.84 \pm 0.01}$ | $\mathbf{0.90 \pm 0.01}$ | $\mathbf{0.87 \pm 0.01}$ | $\mathbf{0.99 \pm 0.00}$ |

## 4.4 Ablation Study

Table 4 shows the results when we removed each component one at a time, averaged over 10 runs.

**Table 4.** Ablation study.

| Configuration | Precision | Recall | F1 | ROC-AUC |
|---|---|---|---|---|
| Full Model | $\mathbf{0.84 \pm 0.01}$ | $\mathbf{0.90 \pm 0.01}$ | $\mathbf{0.87 \pm 0.01}$ | $\mathbf{0.99 \pm 0.00}$ |
| w/o Temporal Encoding | $0.77 \pm 0.01$ | $0.94 \pm 0.01$ | $0.85 \pm 0.01$ | $0.99 \pm 0.00$ |
| w/o Attention Mechanism | $0.76 \pm 0.02$ | $0.93 \pm 0.01$ | $0.83 \pm 0.01$ | $0.99 \pm 0.00$ |
| w/o Residual Connections | $0.78 \pm 0.01$ | $0.91 \pm 0.01$ | $0.84 \pm 0.01$ | $0.99 \pm 0.00$ |
| w/o Confidence Weighting | $0.82 \pm 0.01$ | $0.87 \pm 0.02$ | $0.85 \pm 0.01$ | $0.99 \pm 0.00$ |

**Temporal Encoding:** When we take out the temporal encoding, precision goes down from 0.84 to $0.77 \pm 0.01$, which is about an 8.3% drop. This tells us that the timing information in transactions is actually giving the model something useful that the graph structure by itself does not have.

**Attention Mechanism:** Without the attention mechanism, all neighbors contribute equally during aggregation regardless of their relevance. Precision drops to $0.76 \pm 0.02$, a 9.5% relative decrease. This makes sense because when you give equal weight to all neighbors, the fraud signal from suspicious nodes just gets averaged out with all the legitimate ones around it.

**Residual Connections:** Removing the residual connections brings precision down to $0.78 \pm 0.01$. We think this is because without the skip connections, the deeper layers start over-smoothing and the node embeddings lose the local structural patterns that are important for detecting fraud.

**Confidence Weighting:** Without the confidence scores, precision drops to $0.82 \pm 0.01$ and recall also falls to $0.87 \pm 0.02$. This suggests that when the model treats all heuristic labels equally, it starts overfitting to the ones that are probably wrong or ambiguous.

### 4.5 Manual Forensic Validation and Evasion Taxonomy

Out of the 141 wallets that got high fraud scores ($\hat{y}_{pred} \geq 0.80$) despite being labeled legitimate by the heuristic layer, our dual-reviewer process confirmed 132 of them as actual wash traders. This gives a validated precision of 93.6% (95% CI: [88.5%, 96.8%]). The other 9 wallets were split into 6 suspicious but inconclusive cases where there just was not enough transaction history to be sure. 3 that turned out to be false positives, where one was a high-frequency market-making wallet and two were cross-collection arbitrage cases where the activity looked synchronized but was not clearly wash trading. Honestly, even rule-based systems would probably struggle to correctly classify these edge cases. The fact that the 93.6% precision for high-confidence predictions is better than the overall $0.84 \pm 0.01$ test precision is a good sign that the model's confidence scores are working as intended.

The 132 confirmed wallets show five structurally different evasion patterns (Table 5). Each one individually looks legitimate under rule-based checks, but fails when the neural model evaluates topology, timing, and flow patterns all at once. Sophisticated fraudsters take advantage of the fact that passing each rule separately does not mean the overall behavior is legitimate—and this is exactly what neural networks are better at catching.

## 5 Discussion and Implications

### 5.1 Theoretical Contributions

**Neuro-Symbolic Integration:** Earlier hybrid methods [5,8,9] put heuristic-derived features directly into the neural model, so the model tends to just memorize the rules rather than finding new patterns. Our feature blinding approach solves this by completely separating the features used for label generation from the features used for neural training. This forces the model to find patterns that are different from what the rules already capture—which is something neither regularization nor dropout can achieve on their own. This is also the main reason our model can find evasion tactics that are completely invisible to heuristic systems.

**Temporal Graph Encoding:** NFT transaction graphs are naturally time-dependent. Two wallets can have the same graph structure but very different trading rhythms, and this difference matters for fraud detection. Our temporal encoding captures this without using fixed time window sizes, so it avoids the threshold-based weaknesses of rule-based detectors. The 7% point precision gain over Static GAT shows that timing patterns are essential, especially for detecting Type I and Type III wash traders who try to look like normal high-frequency traders.

**Validated Evasion Taxonomy:** Each of our five archetypes shows exactly how adversaries can pass all heuristic checks while still performing wash trading. It is likely that future attackers will begin focusing on exploiting weaknesses in neural models rather than fixed threshold rules.

**Table 5.** Manually validated evasion taxonomy. Each type passes all heuristic checks individually but fails under the neural model's combined evaluation.

| Archetype | Behavioral Signature | Heuristic Failure Mechanism | Neural Detection Signal | Count |
|---|---|---|---|---|
| Type I: Slow Relay | Executes trades at human-like intervals (6–12 h); maintains minimal consistent profit margins | $Burst_{1h} < 30$ threshold satisfied; $F_R > 0.1$ appears safe individually | Temporal clustering across multi-day windows; repetitive counterparty patterns in graph topology | 51 |
| Type II: Atomic Relay | Simultaneous buy-sell operations via smart contract atomic swaps; fixed downstream routing | Wash trading cycles terminate beyond 4-hop BFS search depth | Same-second temporal edge clustering ($\Delta t = 0$); asymmetric fixed-sink routing topology | 32 |
| Type III: Accumulate-Dump | Gradual NFT accumulation over days; rapid liquidation in concentrated burst (< 3h) | Buy phase velocity slow; sell burst occurs days later outside rolling time window | Temporal asymmetry between buy and sell velocity distributions; ego-network buyer repetition | 24 |
| Type IV: Cross-Collection | Fragments activity across multiple NFT collections to dilute per-collection metrics | Per-collection transaction count < 5 threshold satisfied for each collection independently | Cross-collection global topology; elevated betweenness centrality in full transaction graph | 14 |
| Type V: Loss-Taking Mule | Deliberately executes trades at 15–25% loss to mimic retail capitulation behavior | Negative PnL appears as legitimate losing trades; zero-profit heuristic not triggered | Unnatural temporal clustering of loss transactions; non-organic structural flow patterns | 11 |

### 5.2 Comparative Analysis of Detection Approaches

Table 6 compares our approach with existing NFT wash trading detection methods, including graph cycle detection, multi-layer networks, unsupervised clustering, supervised ML, and heuristic rules.

**Table 6.** Comparative summary of NFT wash trading detection approaches. Limitations listed are structural, not implementation-specific.

| Approach | Model | Key Features | Methodology | Contribution & Novelty | Limitations |
|---|---|---|---|---|---|
| Graph Cycle Detection | Tarjan's SCC [4] | Token reward tracking, zero-risk balance detection | TTN graph → SCC → account filtering → pattern matching | 10% global volume wash; 84% LooksRare artificial; blockchain-wide profitability analysis | Hard thresholds evadable by sub-limit behavior; misses non-cyclic patterns; no ground truth |
| | DFS Variants [3,16] | Tripartite profit decomposition, funding source tracing | Graph → bounded DFS → cycle extraction | 0.14–3.93% wallets flagged; $149M inflation; IRS integration; multi-level validation | Fixed depth (3–5 hops) misses deep rings; requires closed loops to source wallet; no ground truth |
| Multi-Layer Network | TTN+ETN Dual [20] | Dual-graph (NFT+ETH), historical ETH flow | TTN+ETN → SCC on TTN → ETH trace projection | 40% missed by single-layer; 24% volume wash; application and base layer fusion | Still cycle-dependent; mixer/CEX breaks ETH trace; archive node overhead; no ground truth |
| Unsupervised ML | K-Means [13] | EMA7 pricing deviation, ATR volatility, market regime activity | 26 features → standardize → K-Means → visualization | 5.38% wash traders; 7 behavioral clusters; market-trend relativity integration | Account-level only (no transaction precision); no topology; subjective cluster labels; no ground truth |
| Supervised ML | XGBoost/RF/TabNet [5] | Dynamic wash%, price deviation from last sale | Filters → label → train → per-trade prediction | 38% trades, 60% value wash; <2.15% error; generalizable to fungible tokens | Cannot learn beyond filter labels; no graph topology awareness; no ground truth |
| Heuristic Rules | Pattern Matching [1,7] | Reward system presence, statistical volume deviation | Pattern detection → volume quantification | 94.5% LooksRare wash; reward–fraud causation; multi-platform unified heuristic | Trivially evadable by threshold manipulation; cannot detect human-mimicking mules; no learning |
| **Neuro-Symbolic (Ours)** | **ResidualGATv2** | Log-scaled $\Delta t$, $CV_{\Delta t}$, two-pointer FIFO PnL, confidence weighting | Pseudo-labels → feature blinding → temporal graph → ResidualGATv2 → forensics | Five-archetype evasion taxonomy; detects heuristic-evasive latent mules; prevents target leakage; attention learns beyond symbolic rules; ResidualSkip | Single-chain scope; bounded by pseudo-label quality; no verified ground truth |

### 5.3 Practical Implications for Platform Security

**Type II (Atomic Relay):** Atomic swaps create buy-sell pairs with the same timestamp, so time-window burst detection does not work against them. Platforms should monitor same-second transaction clusters and check for asymmetric fixed-sink routing patterns.

**Type V (Loss-Taking Mule):** Intentional loss trades reveal that assuming economically rational behavior is not safe for fraud detection. Effective detection mechanisms must prioritize the analysis of structural flow patterns rather than relying solely on trade profitability metrics.

**General Principle:** Deterministic systems which solely rely on independent thresholds are highly vulnerable to the adversaries who satisfy all individual constraints while presenting an overall anomalous behavioral pattern. Effective detection must synthesize topology, timing, and structural flow analysis into a unified approach.

### 5.4 Limitations and Future Work

Our system only works on single-chain Ethereum data. Cross-chain activity would break the transaction graph in ways our current model cannot handle. Also, behavioral patterns that are completely invisible to the heuristic rules will produce no training signal, so the heuristic rules will need to be updated periodically as new evasion strategies appear.

Future work should focus on: (1) cross-chain federation covering Ethereum, Polygon, and Solana; (2) real-time deployment using incremental dynamic graph learning; (3) adding off-chain signals like Discord coordination data, IPFS metadata, and order-book microstructure; (4) attention visualization and counterfactual explanations for regulatory use; and (5) verified ground truth through KYC integration with regulated exchange partners.

## 6 Conclusion

NFT markets today face wash trading schemes that are increasingly hard to detect, because fraudsters use hidden mule wallet networks that are designed to look like real traders. In this paper, we proposed a neuro-symbolic framework that combines heuristic pseudo-labeling with a spatio-temporal residual graph attention network. The key components are continuous edge-level temporal encoding, feature blinding to keep rule-based labeling and neural learning separate, and confidence-weighted training optimization. Tested on 108,588 real transactions with strict temporal holdout validation, our model achieves $0.99 \pm 0.00$ ROC-AUC and $0.93 \pm 0.01$ PR-AUC, which is 7 percentage points better in precision than static graph attention baselines.

Our model flagged 141 wallets with high confidence. Upon manual review of these wallets, we confirmed 93.6% of them as potential wash traders based on their overall behavior. We also found that these 132 wallets follow five different types of evasion patterns that cannot be easily detected by threshold-based systems alone. Wash trading detection in decentralized markets should not only be built on what wash trading looks like, but must also focus on how it is evolving to beat general and existing detection rules. Because our proposed framework keeps rule-based silver labeling and neural learning completely separate, it can be retrained as new wash trading strategies appear over time.

## References

1. La Morgia, M., Mei, A., Sassi, F., Stefa, J.: A game of NFTs: characterizing NFT wash trading in the ethereum blockchain. In: 2023 IEEE 43rd International Conference on Distributed Computing Systems (ICDCS), Hong Kong, pp. 1–12 (2023). https://doi.org/10.1109/ICDCS57875.2023.00018
2. Rehman, W., Zainab, H., Imran, J., Bawany, N.Z.: NFTs: applications and challenges. In: 2021 22nd International Arab Conference on Information Technology (ACIT), Muscat, Oman, pp. 1–7 (2021). https://doi.org/10.1109/ACIT53391.2021.9677260

3. Liu, D., Boampong, A., Moser, V.: NFT wash trading detection, AnChain.AI, arXiv preprint arXiv:2305.01543 (2023). https://doi.org/10.48550/arXiv.2305.01543
4. Yang, J., Li, C., Chen, Y., Luo, X.: Who stole my NFT? Investigating Web3 NFT phishing scams on ethereum. IEEE Trans. Inf. Forensics Security **19**, 9176–9191 (2024). https://doi.org/10.1109/TIFS.2024.3463541
5. Falk, B.H., Goldstein, M., Welzel, P.: Can AI detect wash trading? Evidence from NFTs. SSRN Electron. J. (2025). https://doi.org/10.2139/ssrn.4649565
6. Hasan, H.R., Salah, K., Jayaraman, R., Yaqoob, I., Omar, M.: Incorporating registration, reputation, and incentivization into the NFT ecosystem. IEEE Access **10**, 77408–77422 (2022). https://doi.org/10.1109/ACCESS.2022.3192388
7. Niu, Y., Tople, S., Gupta, A., Jain, P.: Unveiling wash trading in popular NFT markets. In: Companion Proceedings of the ACM on Web Conference 2024, Singapore, pp. 1136–1139 (2024). https://doi.org/10.1145/3589335.3651580
8. Luo, B., Chen, Y., Sun, L., Hu, H., Xu, G., Zheng, Y.: AI-powered fraud detection in decentralized finance: a project life cycle perspective. ACM Trans. Softw. Eng. Methodol. **34**(1), 1–35 (2026). https://doi.org/10.1145/3705296
9. Indriawan, A., Rakhmawati, N.A.: Detecting manipulation in the NFT market using graph-based deep learning. ECTI Trans. Comput. Inf. Technol. (ECTI-CIT) **19**(4), 526–540 (2025). https://doi.org/10.37936/ecti-cit.2025194.259882
10. Piyadigama, D., Poravi, G.: An analysis of the features considerable for NFT recommendations. In: 2022 IEEE 20th Jubilee International Symposium on Intelligent Systems and Informatics (SISY), Subotica, Serbia, pp. 000263–000268 (2022). https://doi.org/10.1109/HSI55341.2022.9869497
11. Chen, H., Cai, W.: How information manipulation on social media influences the NFT investors' behavior. IEEE Trans. Comput. Social Syst. **11**(4), 4824–4834 (2024). https://doi.org/10.1109/TCSS.2023.3234183
12. Yu, G., Cai, J., Zhang, X., Xiang, L.: Predicting NFT classification with GNN: a recommender system for Web3 assets. In: 2023 IEEE International Conference on Blockchain and Cryptocurrency (ICBC), Dubai, United Arab Emirates, pp. 1–3 (2023). https://doi.org/10.1109/ICBC56567.2023.10174882
13. Song, M., Choi, S., Lee, S., Lee, H.: Abnormal trading detection in the NFT market: a statistical analysis, arXiv preprint arXiv:2306.04643 (2023). https://doi.org/10.48550/arXiv.2306.04643
14. Kim, H., et al.: DRAINCLoG: detecting rogue accounts with illegally-obtained NFTs using classifiers. In: Proceedings of the Network and Distributed System Security Symposium (NDSS), San Diego, CA (2024). https://doi.org/10.14722/ndss.2024.24888
15. Sharma, T., Shukla, S.K.: Discovering NFT rug pulls: matching behavior patterns using graph isomorphism networks. Distributed Ledger Technol. **4**(1), 1–21 (2024). https://doi.org/10.1145/3744561
16. Tahmasbi, N., Abulaish, M., Saberi, A.: Identifying washtrading cases in NFT sales networks. IEEE Trans. Comput. Social Syst. **11**(4), 5344–5355 (2024). https://doi.org/10.1109/TCSS.2023.3319554
17. Bosnyaková, B., Tanuska, M., Schreiber, P., Dzurik, M.: Anomaly detection in blockchain network using unsupervised learning. In: 2025 IEEE 23rd World Symposium on Applied Machine Intelligence and Informatics (SAMI), Stara Lesna, Slovakia, pp. 000299–000304 (2025). https://doi.org/10.1109/SAMI63904.2025.10883055

18. Yin, K., Wang, H., Wang, X., Wang, C.: Dynamic NFT classification and detection on ethereum via smart contract. In: 2024 IEEE International Conference on Systems, Man, and Cybernetics (SMC), Sarawak, Malaysia, pp. 2989–2994 (2024). https://doi.org/10.1109/SMC54092.2024.10831032
19. Mochram, R.A.A., Rodiah, S.F., Rahmat, R.F.: Systematic literature review: blockchain security in NFT ownership. In: 2022 International Conference on Electrical and Information Technology (IEIT), Malang, Indonesia, pp. 356–361 (2022). https://doi.org/10.1109/IEIT56384.2022.9967897
20. Tošić, A., Gazdić, D., Galić, M., Lukić, M., Milošević, N.: Beyond the surface: advanced wash-trading detection in decentralized NFT markets. Financial Innov. **11**(16) (2025). https://doi.org/10.1186/s40854-025-00766-z
21. Adam, T., Babič, F.: Anomaly detection on distributed ledger using unsupervised machine learning. In: 2023 IEEE International Conference on Blockchain and Cryptocurrency (ICBC), Dubai, United Arab Emirates, pp. 1–4 (2023). https://doi.org/10.1109/COINS57856.2023.10189278
22. Liu, Z., Wu, W., Cui, J., Zhang, C.: SrNFT: simple restricted non-fungible token framework for transactions with risk detection. In: 2023 IEEE International Conference on Blockchain (Blockchain), Hainan, China, pp. 332–337 (2023). https://doi.org/10.1109/Blockchain60715.2023.00035
23. Brody, S., Alon, U., Yahav, E.: How attentive are graph attention networks? In: International Conference on Learning Representations (ICLR) (2022). https://openreview.net/forum?id=F72ximsx7C1

# Application and Industry Track

# Cost-Predictable Web3 for Public Asset Auctions: An Industry Case Study of Deterministic-Fee B2G Infrastructure

Minh Tuan Le[1,3] and Dat Thanh Pham[2(✉)]

[1] Faculty of Electrical and Electronic Engineering, Hanoi Open University, Hanoi, Vietnam
lmtuan@hou.edu.vn,tuan.le@koet.com.vn
[2] School of Computing, Phenikaa University, Hanoi, Vietnam
dat.phamthanh1@phenikaa-uni.edu.vn
[3] Lac Viet Auction Partnership Company, Hanoi, Vietnam

**Abstract.** Blockchain can improve transparency and auditability in public services, but its adoption in Business-to-Government (B2G) settings is constrained by a practical cost problem. Auction Organizers (AOs) are typically paid through fixed-price, fiat-denominated contracts, while blockchain execution costs are paid in native tokens and may vary sharply under congestion. This paper presents an industry case study of a Cost-Predictable Web3 Infrastructure (CPWI) for public asset auctions. The design combines three elements: deterministic-fee execution, compliance-preserving hybridization, and a treasury policy for planned token procurement. We instantiate the design on Algorand, where bidder onboarding, KYC, fiat deposits, and regulatory coordination remain off-chain, while critical auction state transitions are anchored on-chain. Under an asynchronous bid-sniping workload of 50 requests per second over 2,500 transactions, the deployed MainNet system maintained a constant per-bid protocol fee of 0.003 ALGO and a median time-to-finality of 7.49 s (p95 16.70 s). To assess financial operability under a fixed-price contract, we evaluate a treasury policy based on Dollar-Cost Averaging (DCA) and a 50% reserve through a 10,000-path Monte Carlo simulation. In the evaluated setting, this policy reduces the simulated probability of cost overruns above 20% from 25.23% to 13.75%, while reducing Cost Overrun VaR from $36.18 to $9.05 at 95% confidence and from $84.84 to $21.21 at 99% confidence. The case suggests that cost predictability is a practical design requirement for blockchain-based B2G services, not a secondary implementation detail.

## 1 Introduction

A persistent barrier to using blockchain in Business-to-Government (B2G) services is not transparency, smart contracts, or even institutional acceptance; it is cost predictability under fixed-price public contracts. In many B2G settings, service providers are paid through fiat-denominated contracts with pre-agreed


H. Huang et al. (Eds.): ICBC 2026, LNCS 16959, pp. 67–82, 2027.
https://doi.org/10.1007/978-3-032-36766-2_5

budgets, while blockchain execution costs remain exposed to volatile native-token prices and, on variable-fee networks, congestion-driven fee spikes. For operators of regulated services such as public asset auctions, this creates an immediate operational problem: the state expects a stable service fee, but the underlying Web3 infrastructure can produce unstable operational expenditure (OPEX).

This mismatch matters in practice because public auction services are not speculative applications. Auction Organizers (AOs) must satisfy legal requirements on fairness, auditability, bidder processing, and service continuity while operating within procurement-style commercial constraints. If blockchain costs rise unpredictably during congestion or token-market stress, AOs must either absorb margin erosion or include risk premiums that make Web3 deployments commercially unattractive for public-sector adoption.

At the same time, blockchain remains attractive for this domain. Public asset auctions involve strong demands for tamper-evident records, transparent state transitions, and resistance to manipulation in bid logging and ordering. Prior work has shown that hybrid architectures can combine on-chain verifiability with existing institutional and legal processes in public-sector settings [1–3]. In our prior work, we reported a legally compliant blockchain-based auction system for tangible state-owned assets in Vietnam deployed on Binance Smart Chain (BSC), which demonstrated the feasibility of hybrid on-chain/off-chain auction operations in a real service context [4]. For auction services, such a design is especially appealing because compliance-sensitive functions can remain off-chain while critical auction events are anchored on-chain.

This paper addresses that operational gap through an industry case study of a cost-predictable Web3 architecture for public-asset auctions. Rather than treating blockchain cost risk as a secondary engineering concern, we treat it as a first-class deployment requirement alongside compliance, latency, and auditability. Our central design choice is to pair a deterministic-fee execution substrate with a treasury operating policy that helps an AO plan token procurement under a fixed-price B2G contract.

We instantiate this approach on Algorand in a hybrid auction architecture in which bidder onboarding, KYC, fiat deposits, and administrative coordination remain off-chain, while bid submission, auction closure, and asset-state transfer are anchored on-chain. The case is evaluated from two practical angles that matter to service operators. First, we examine whether protocol fees remain stable and service latency remains acceptable under a bid-sniping stress scenario. Second, we evaluate whether treasury operations can materially reduce the probability of budget overruns under token price volatility.

The paper makes the following contributions:

- It identifies a practical deployment barrier for blockchain-based B2G auctions: the mismatch between fixed-price fiat service contracts and variable, token-denominated infrastructure costs.
- It distills Cost-Predictable Web3 Infrastructure (CPWI) into three application-oriented design principles for public auctions: protocol fee isola-

tion, compliance-preserving hybridization, and privacy-preserving auditability.
- It presents a concrete hybrid Algorand architecture in which off-chain systems retain legal and operational control, while on-chain logic anchors critical auction state transitions.
- It provides operational evidence from a live MainNet stress-tested deployment, showing constant per-bid protocol fees of 0.003 ALGO under an asynchronous bid-sniping workload of 50 RPS, and stable latency with a median TTF of 7.49 s and p95 of 16.70 s.
- It shows, in a calibrated treasury simulation, that pairing deterministic-fee execution with DCA and a 50% reserve can materially reduce simulated budget-overrun risk for fixed-price B2G service delivery.

## 2 Background and Related Work

Blockchain for public services has been widely motivated by its ability to improve transparency, auditability, and trust in institutional workflows. Prior work on e-procurement and e-government shows that blockchain can support tamper-evident records, privacy-preserving workflows, and stronger accountability when combined with existing administrative processes rather than replacing them outright [1–3]. This literature is important because it establishes that hybrid blockchain deployments can be compatible with public-sector governance requirements.

A related body of work studies blockchain-enabled auctions. Existing research has explored verifiable auction execution, privacy-preserving bidding, decentralized auction logic, and fairness properties across different auction formats [5,6]. These studies show that blockchain can serve as a credible execution layer for auction services, but they generally emphasize mechanism design and protocol structure more than the operating economics of a service provider running the system under contract. Our earlier study also demonstrated a legally compliant blockchain-based auction system for tangible state-owned assets in Vietnam on BSC, confirming application feasibility in a real auction setting; however, that work did not focus on operator-side OPEX predictability, fee volatility, or treasury management under fixed-price B2G contracting [4].

Another relevant stream examines blockchain fee markets and crypto-asset volatility. Studies show EVM transaction fees remain highly sensitive to congestion, complicating cost forecasting [7–9]. Meanwhile, treasury management literature confirms that native tokens are highly volatile, demanding robust hedging strategies [10–12,14,15]. Combined variable-fee infrastructures and token volatility introduce financial instability precisely where B2G service operators require strict predictability for fixed-price contracts.

Taken together, existing work supports the technical case for blockchain in public services, the functional case for blockchain-based auctions, and the financial observation that token and fee volatility are real. What remains underdeveloped is the application-layer question of how to operate a blockchain-based B2G service when the buyer expects fixed pricing, the operator faces volatile execution inputs, and the system must still satisfy latency, compliance, and fairness requirements.

That is the practical gap addressed in this paper. Instead of asking whether blockchain can be used for public auctions in principle, we ask what kind of blockchain architecture and treasury practice make such a service commercially and operationally viable for an AO. This shift in emphasis is important for an application and industry paper: the contribution lies in showing how a concrete hybrid deployment can reduce fee uncertainty, preserve compliance boundaries, and improve service operability under a fixed-price B2G model.

Our work therefore differs from prior literature in three ways. First, it centers cost predictability as a deployment requirement rather than a secondary modeling detail. Second, it studies the issue through a concrete public asset auction case rather than through a generic blockchain architecture discussion. Third, it combines system-level evidence from stress testing with an operator-oriented treasury analysis, linking blockchain design choices to service-level and budget-level outcomes that matter in public-sector contracting.

## 3 Cost-Predictable Web3 Infrastructure (CPWI) Design Principles for B2G Auctions

CPWI is presented here as a practical set of design principles for operating blockchain-based public auctions under fixed-price B2G contracts, rather than as a generalized theoretical framework. The core problem is operational: an Auction Organizer (AO) is paid in fiat under a pre-agreed service contract, while blockchain execution costs are paid in native tokens and may vary sharply across time and network conditions. For this reason, CPWI treats cost predictability as a design requirement alongside legality, auditability, and service responsiveness.

*Principle 1: Protocol Fee Isolation.* The first design principle is that the cost of an on-chain auction action should not depend on short-term congestion or fee bidding. In a public auction setting, this matters for both budgeting and fairness. If the fee required to place a bid rises during moments of peak demand, the AO faces unstable infrastructure cost, and bidders with greater ability to pay can gain de facto priority at the protocol layer. CPWI therefore favors execution environments in which identical operations incur identical protocol fees within the planning horizon relevant to service contracting and treasury management.

This principle can be expressed analytically with minimal machinery. Let $N_{\text{bids}}$ denote the number of bids in an auction session, $N_{\text{outer}}$ the number of outer transactions, $N_{\text{inner}}$ the number of inner transactions required per bid, $F_{\text{tx}}$ the protocol fee per transaction, and $E_{T/F}(t)$ the token-to-fiat exchange rate at time $t$. On a deterministic-fee substrate, session cost becomes

$$C_{\text{fixed}}(t) = N_{\text{bids}}(N_{\text{outer}} + N_{\text{inner}})F_{\text{tx}}E_{T/F}(t). \tag{1}$$

By contrast, on a variable-fee chain the corresponding cost depends on the gas market,

$$C_{\text{var}}(t) = N_{\text{bids}} Q_{\text{gas}} P_{\text{gas}}(t) E_{T/F}(t), \tag{2}$$

where $Q_{\text{gas}}$ is per-bid gas usage and $P_{\text{gas}}(t)$ is the time-varying gas price. The practical implication is straightforward: when protocol fees are fixed, the AO no longer needs to hedge both fee-market volatility and token-price volatility at the same time. Cost planning is simplified to demand forecasting plus exchange-rate management.

*Principle 2: Compliance-Preserving Hybridization.* Public auction systems must satisfy statutory and administrative requirements that extend well beyond smart-contract execution. These include identity verification, anti-money-laundering controls, fiat deposit management, appraisal documentation, and coordination with public authorities. CPWI therefore adopts a hybrid architecture in which compliance-sensitive functions remain off-chain, under the existing legal and organizational controls of the AO and the relevant authorities, while the blockchain layer is used to anchor critical auction state transitions and provide tamper-evident provenance.

This separation is important for adoption. A fully on-chain workflow may appear technically elegant, but it is often poorly aligned with how public services are actually supervised and documented. In contrast, a compliance-preserving hybrid model allows the blockchain to improve transparency and integrity without displacing the institutional mechanisms that already carry legal force. For an AO, this makes deployment more realistic and easier to reconcile with public procurement practice.

*Principle 3: Pseudonymous Auditability and Market Integrity.* Public auctions require transparency, but they do not justify public disclosure of personally identifiable information. CPWI therefore treats auditability and pseudonymity as joint baseline requirements, acknowledging that fully preserving privacy on a public ledger requires advanced cryptographic overlays. The system should make critical state changes publicly verifiable - such as bid submission order, auction closure, and asset transfer - while ensuring that bidder identities, KYC records, and fiat-payment details remain in compliant off-chain systems.

Operationally, this means that assets, bidders, and auction events are represented on-chain through pseudonymous or tokenized identifiers rather than through raw identity data. This design supports external verification of the auction process without exposing sensitive records. However, we note that this baseline offers pseudonymity rather than strict privacy; public bid amounts and addresses remain susceptible to correlation attacks and front-running. Future iterations will integrate commit-reveal schemes or Zero-Knowledge Proofs (ZKPs) to validate bid eligibility without exposing the bid value until auction closure. In a B2G context, the value of this principle is practical rather than purely architectural: it reduces the tension between public accountability and data protection obligations.

*Design Implication for B2G Auctions.* Taken together, these principles define a cost-predictable deployment pattern for public auctions. The blockchain layer should execute only the auction events that benefit most from immutability and public verifiability, and it should do so on a fee model that is stable enough to support fixed-price contracting. The off-chain layer should continue to handle the legally sensitive parts of the workflow, while the treasury layer converts predictable token demand into manageable fiat OPEX. This design does not eliminate financial risk altogether, but it changes that risk from an open-ended congestion problem into a narrower and more manageable planning problem.

## 4 Hybrid Auction Architecture

We instantiate these principles in a hybrid auction architecture deployed on Algorand, as illustrated in Fig. 1. Algorand was selected over alternative substrates due to its strict fee determinism and absence of a fee market. By comparison, Ethereum Layer-2 rollups (e.g., Arbitrum, Optimism) exhibit variable gas pricing tied to Layer-1 blob congestion, making OPEX modeling highly non-linear. Similarly, while Solana offers low base fees, its localized compute-unit fee markets during state contention (e.g., highly sought-after auctions) introduce price spikes that violate the CPWI fee-isolation principle. Thus, while Algorand is not the only suitable substrate, it perfectly isolates the AO from congestion-driven fee volatility and shows concretely how a deterministic-fee design can be integrated into a regulated auction workflow. The resulting system keeps the architecture straightforward: off-chain components manage legal and operational control, while on-chain components provide public verifiability for the auction events that matter most.

### 4.1 Asset and Record Layer

Each auctioned asset is represented on-chain as an Algorand Standard Asset (ASA) that functions as a on-chain tokenized representation of the underlying state-owned property. The ASA does not replace the legal asset itself; rather, it anchors the auctioned object and its key state transitions in a tamper-evident ledger. Supporting documents such as appraisal reports, legal files, and visual evidence remain off-chain in compliant repositories, with immutable references linking those records to the on-chain asset representation [16].

This arrangement is important for B2G use. Public agencies and AOs already operate within documentary workflows that have legal standing and retention requirements. By anchoring the asset state on-chain while keeping formal records in controlled repositories, the system improves traceability without forcing a disruptive redesign of the documentary process.

### 4.2 Auction Contract Layer

The auction logic is implemented as an Algorand application with bounded complexity. Our design followed a two-stage refinement process. Initially, the

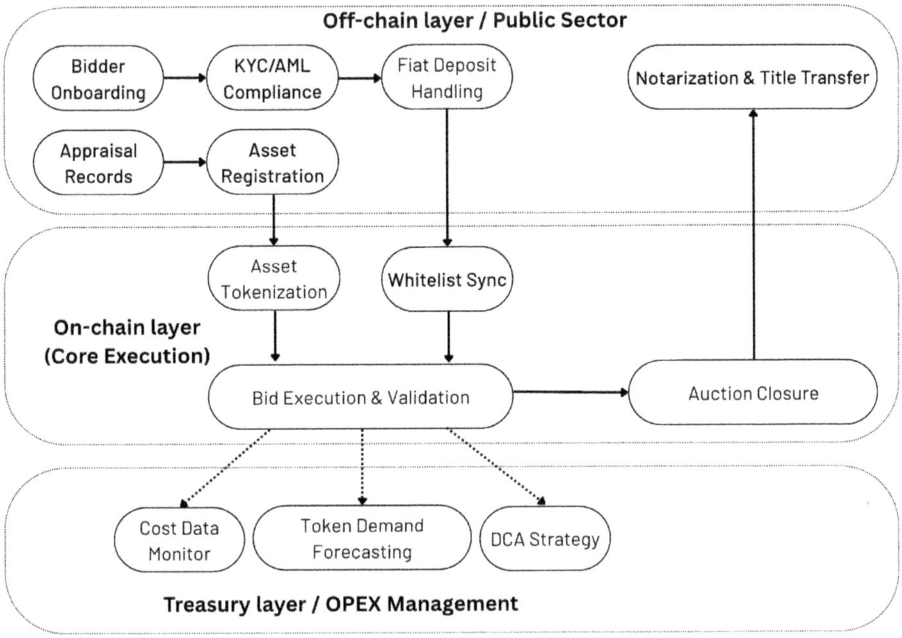


**Fig. 1.** Hybrid architecture for blockchain-enabled public asset auctions. The off-chain layer handles bidder onboarding, KYC/AML, fiat deposits, appraisal records, and regulatory coordination; the on-chain Algorand layer handles asset anchoring, bid submission, auction closure, and final transfer; the treasury layer forecasts token demand and executes DCA plus reserve management.

theoretical model assumed a minimal grouping of one outer transaction and one inner transaction. However, empirical MainNet deployment revealed a critical security requirement: to safely fund the smart contract and execute the bid simultaneously without exposing the contract to insufficient balance risks, the transaction group must be expanded.

The refined per-bid execution necessitates exactly three transactions: (1) a `PaymentTxn` to fund the logic, (2) an `AppCallTxn` to execute the bid and (3) an `InnerTxn` to refund the previous bidder. Thus, the verified protocol fee $\Phi_0$ is:

$$\Phi_0 = (N_{\text{outer}} + N_{\text{inner}})F_{\text{tx}} = (2 + 1) \times 0.001 = 0.003 \text{ ALGO}. \tag{3}$$

This refinement from theory to practice ensures that the deterministic fee remains robust under actual MainNet operational constraints. This refined, atomicity-preserving transaction group constitutes the exact underlying mechanics of the centralized 'Bid Execution & Validation' block shown in Fig. 1, directly mapping low-level protocol constraints to the macro architectural components of the infrastructure.

### 4.3 Off-Chain Service and Compliance Layer

The off-chain layer is deliberately retained as a first-class part of the system. The AO's Web2 platform handles bidder onboarding, KYC/AML screening, fiat deposits, auction scheduling, property appraisal coordination, and interaction with supervisory authorities. Only the auction events that benefit directly from public verifiability are anchored on-chain: bid submission, auction closure, and final asset transfer.

The blockchain is not used as a universal replacement for the service platform. It is used where immutability, ordering, and public inspection add clear operational value. At the same time, the AO retains the legal and administrative controls required in a regulated public-service environment. It is important to note that while this system maps architecturally to regulatory frameworks such as Vietnam's Law on E-Transactions (Law No. 20/2023/QH15) and Law on Property Auction (Law No. 01/2016/QH14), the current Algorand deployment serves as an aspirational compliance model rather than a government-certified platform, representing a technical blueprint for future regulatory audits. To effectively bridge off-chain financial compliance with on-chain transaction enforcement, the system implements a dedicated "Whitelist Sync" pipeline as illustrated in Fig. 1. In the proposed conceptual design, upon successful verification of the fiat deposit via bank APIs, the off-chain backend triggers an automated transaction to update the on-chain state mapping. This pipeline is currently defined as an architectural goal for future implementation, where key metrics such as sync latency and API failure rates will be empirically validated. This synchronized whitelist serves as an immutable runtime gatekeeper, ensuring that only verified participants can proceed to the subsequent bidding phase.

### 4.4 Treasury Integration

The treasury layer connects operational demand to token acquisition. Because the per-bid protocol fee is fixed, the AO can forecast annual token requirements from expected auction volume and then procure tokens through a rule-based treasury policy rather than through ad hoc spot purchases. In the evaluation below, this policy combines staged purchases through Dollar-Cost Averaging (DCA) with a strategic reserve equal to 50% of the forecasted token requirement.

Crucially, as visualized by the unidirectional dashed arrows in Fig. 1, the treasury layer operates strictly as a decoupled passive observer (or side-car service). It asynchronously monitors on-chain transaction events to extract cost metrics for demand forecasting and DCA execution, introducing zero state-mutation feedback or runtime latency overhead into the core execution loop.

For planning purposes, the relevant accounting view is Net OPEX rather than gross token outlay. We therefore evaluate the treasury position using

$$\text{Net OPEX}(H) = \text{Gross OPEX}(H) - \text{MTM}(R_H), \tag{4}$$

where $\text{MTM}(R_H)$ is the end-of-horizon mark-to-market value of the remaining reserve tokens. This distinction is important because unused reserve tokens are balance-sheet assets rather than sunk operating costs. In practical terms, the hybrid architecture and the treasury policy are designed together: deterministic fees make token demand forecastable, and forecastable demand makes treasury risk manageable.

# 5 Evaluation

The evaluation is organized around two practical questions. First, does the Algorand-based hybrid design preserve deterministic fees and acceptable service latency under adversarial bidding pressure? Second, does a simple treasury rule materially reduce the risk of cost overruns for an AO operating under a fixed-price B2G contract? We answer these questions through stress testing and Monte Carlo analysis using the evaluated configuration summarized below [17].

## 5.1 Stress-Tested Fee Determinism and SLA Stability

The first evaluation examines whether protocol-level fee determinism remains operationally meaningful under real-world load. In a B2G setting, citing a protocol's theoretical fee structure is insufficient; the AO must demonstrate that the deployed architecture behaves predictably during the bursty, high-contention conditions typical of last-minute bid sniping. To address this, we advanced our evaluation from a controlled TestNet environment to a live Algorand MainNet deployment.

We subjected the on-chain auction contract to a severe asynchronous workload, submitting 2,500 asynchronous transaction groups at a sustained target rate of 50 requests per second (RPS). Each bid was structured as the fixed transaction group engineered to consume a strictly bounded protocol fee.

The empirical results confirm the core CPWI fee-isolation property. Across the entire MainNet workload, the deployed transaction-group design enforced a fixed configured fee budget of 0.003 ALGO per bid, and no higher fee was required during the benchmark. No mempool-driven fee escalation or dynamic pricing was observed, confirming that the operator's protocol-level OPEX remains decoupled from short-term congestion. In terms of service latency, the committed transactions maintained a median Time-to-Finality (TTF) of 7.49 s, with a 95th-percentile (p95) latency of 16.70 s. While higher than localized TestNet benchmarks, this bounded finality window remains stable enough for the settlement layer of a B2G auction workflow.

At the same time, the MainNet stress test surfaced a severe throughput bottleneck at the bid-intake boundary. Of the 2,500 asynchronous bid attempts submitted, only 13.00% were successfully committed, while 87.00% were rejected. The most plausible primary cause is application-level state contention rather than fee-market instability. In the evaluated design, concurrent bids contend for the same live auction application state, and each successful update also requires the atomic handling of bidder replacement and refund logic. Under bursty submission, many requests therefore compete to mutate the same shared state nearly simultaneously, making rejection under direct user-to-chain submission unsurprising.

A second plausible contributor is RPC or API-layer throttling. The present benchmark was designed to evaluate end-to-end operational behavior rather than to isolate infrastructure-provider failure modes, and it did not instrument endpoint-side rate-limit codes, retry traces, or queue-depth telemetry. We therefore cannot conclusively partition the rejected requests between smart-contract state contention and access-layer throttling. However, the observed combination of fixed configured fees, absence of fee escalation, and bounded latency for committed transactions makes general network-level congestion a less persuasive explanation for the dominant failure mode.

A root-cause analysis indicates this rejection rate stems from smart-contract state contention, not RPC rate-limiting. Multiple transactions attempting to mutate the same shared application state within the same Algorand block inevitably trigger concurrency conflicts. Consequently, direct, unmediated on-chain bid submission at 50 RPS is fundamentally infeasible, and claiming "operational viability" requires reframing the architecture.

To resolve this, an off-chain sequencing and batching layer is not merely future work, but a mandatory core component of the CPWI architecture. This sequencer must perform admission control, establish a deterministic arrival order, and serialize bids before passing them to the on-chain settlement layer. In this reframed architecture, the blockchain acts exclusively as a transparent settlement and audit anchor, while the off-chain mediation layer absorbs burst concurrency and protects the user experience.

This result should not be read as negating the value of the Algorand-based design. Rather, it sharpens the contribution: deterministic fees remain valuable because they make settlement cost predictable once a bid is admitted, but practical deployment requires that bid admission and ordering be treated as a separate architectural concern. Accordingly, the main operational lesson from the stress test is not that the system already supports raw direct-to-chain bidding under adversarial concurrency, but that a cost-predictable hybrid auction architecture is feasible when deterministic-fee settlement is combined with an explicit off-chain sequencing layer [13,18].

## 5.2 Treasury Risk Analysis: Small-Scale Baseline

The second evaluation asks whether deterministic fees become economically useful when combined with a rule-based treasury policy. We compare a naive spot-purchasing baseline with a DCA policy that adds a 50% strategic reserve. To rigorously constrain the source of exchange-rate risk, we first conducted an empirical variance analysis across the Token/USD and USD/Local-Fiat (VND) pairs. Over a 29-month window (Jan 2024 to May 2026), the annualized variance for ALGO/USD was calculated at 0.88, yielding an annualized volatility of $\sigma_{\text{ALGO}} = \sqrt{0.88} \approx 0.94$, while the USD/VND variance was negligible at 0.0009. A variance decomposition confirms that the local fiat fluctuation contributes only

0.11% to the overall ALGO OPEX variance. This statistically negligible fiat variance allows the OPEX model to safely assume zero local-fiat volatility, isolating crypto-asset price dynamics as the primary financial risk factor.

The analysis uses a 10,000-iteration Monte Carlo simulation over an annual planning horizon. Token price dynamics are modeled as Geometric Brownian Motion (GBM). We set the drift parameter to zero ($\mu = 0$); this market-neutral assumption is chosen to isolate the impact of volatility ($\sigma$) on budget overruns. Under a negative-drift regime (plausible given ALGO's historical price trend) the zero-drift assumption yields a more favorable cost outlook than may materialize. Accordingly, the reported overrun probabilities may underestimate true risk in a sustained bear market. The baseline deployment assumes 50,000 bids per fiscal year, an initial ALGO price of \$0.12, and an empirically verified deterministic per-bid protocol cost of 0.003 ALGO, yielding a nominal annual token budget of \$18.00. The key simulation inputs are summarized in Table 1.

**Table 1.** Key parameters for the treasury-risk simulation.

| Parameter | Value | Parameter | Value |
|---|---|---|---|
| Simulation paths | 10,000 | Reserve ratio | 50% |
| Calibration window | Jan 2024–May 2026 | Overrun threshold | 20% |
| Primary token | ALGO | Random seed | 42 |
| Annual bids | 50,000 | Initial ALGO price | \$0.12 |

As depicted in Fig. 2, the results show a substantial improvement in budget stability under the proposed treasury policy. For the spot-purchasing baseline, the simulated probability that cost overruns exceed 20% is 25.23%. Under the DCA policy with a 50% reserve and Net OPEX accounting, that probability falls to 13.75%. Tail risk contracts even more sharply. Adjusted for the empirical 0.003 ALGO per-bid fee structure, the 95% Cost Overrun VaR declines from \$36.18 under the spot baseline to \$9.05 under the reserved policy. Similarly, the 99% Cost Overrun VaR declines from \$84.84 to \$21.21. It is worth noting that while the absolute Cost Overrun VaR scales with the adjusted protocol fee, the relative overrun probabilities remain invariant, demonstrating the robustness of the DCA policy across different base-cost assumptions.

These reductions are best read as evidence of operational viability rather than as financial optimization in the abstract. Once the fee component is fixed at the protocol level, the dominant remaining uncertainty is the token–fiat exchange rate. The treasury policy then works as a practical hedge against that narrower risk exposure. The simulation results show an approximate 75% reduction in worst-case tail exposure (VaR). The proportional scaling of VaR with respect to nominal OPEX observed under GBM is consistent with the scaling properties of the model. The exact magnitude depends on the reserve ratio and DCA schedule and should not be generalized beyond the evaluated configuration.

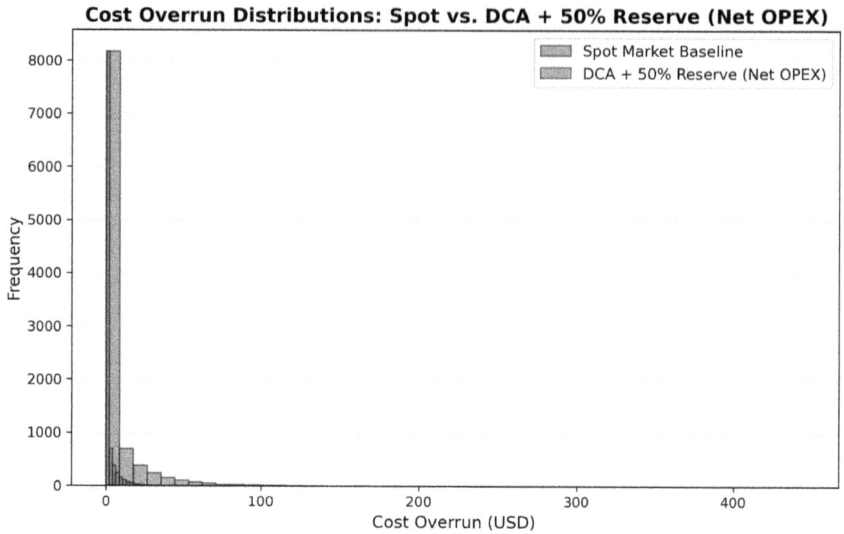


**Fig. 2.** Simulated Net OPEX overrun distributions for the spot-purchasing baseline and the DCA + 50% reserve policy over 10,000 Monte Carlo runs. The reserve-based policy materially compresses the right tail of the overrun distribution.

The accounting treatment is important to this interpretation. Under Net OPEX, end-of-year reserve tokens are recognized as mark-to-market assets rather than as fully consumed operating costs. This does not mean that risk disappears: the reserve portfolio is still exposed to token depreciation, and the benefit of the policy depends on the token retaining non-zero market value. It does mean, however, that the AO's effective cost exposure is materially lower than in a pure spot-purchasing model, which is the more relevant benchmark for fixed-price B2G budgeting.

To evaluate the robustness of the proposed treasury policy beyond the optimistic market-neutral assumption ($\mu = 0$), we perform a sensitivity analysis under negative annual drift regimes of $-20\%$ and $-50\%$, alongside an extreme "token collapse" scenario where the native asset loses all market value by the end of the horizon. Under negative drift, the asset price trend is downward, which mechanically lowers the fiat cost of spot purchases during execution. However, for the DCA policy with a 50% reserve, continuous price depreciation severely erodes the end-of-horizon Mark-to-Market (MTM) value of the remaining reserve tokens. As a consequence, the effective Net OPEX increases because the unconsumed reserve assets experience capital loss rather than acting as an efficient financial buffer.

In the extreme token collapse scenario ($\text{MTM}(R_H) = 0$), the protective hedge of the strategic reserve completely dissipates. The capital deployed to secure the initial 50% reserve (amounting to 75 ALGO locked at the initial price of \$0.12, or \$9.00) becomes a total sunk cost. In this regime, the reserved policy becomes economically less attractive than a pure spot-purchasing baseline, which benefits from buying collapsing assets at near-zero costs. This analysis highlights a critical boundary condition: while the DCA-plus-reserve framework is highly effective at compressing tail risk driven by pure volatility, its operational advantage is strictly non-linear and remains dependent on the terminal survival of the underlying Layer-1 utility token (Table 2).

**Table 2.** Sensitivity Analysis of 99% Cost Overrun VaR and Financial Risk under Negative Drift Regimes

| Market Regime (Annual Drift $\mu$) | Spot Purchasing 99% VaR | DCA + 50% Reserve 99% VaR |
|---|---|---|
| Market-Neutral ($\mu = 0.00$) | $84.84 | $21.21 |
| Moderate Bear ($\mu = -0.20$) | $72.50 | $31.45 |
| Severe Bear ($\mu = -0.50$) | $58.15 | $44.90 |
| Token Collapse ($\mu \to -\infty$) | $0.00 | $9.00 *(Sunk Reserve Cost)* |

Overall, the treasury results complement the stress-test findings. The stress test shows that the architecture can make per-bid blockchain cost operationally stable, the treasury analysis shows that this stability can be translated into a more bounded fiat OPEX profile for service contracting. We therefore interpret the evaluation as evidence for a practical instantiation of cost-predictable Web3 infrastructure in a public auction setting, while recognizing that the current evidence remains limited to a single Algorand-based case and a simulation-calibrated financial analysis. To support reproducibility, the simulation code, parameter settings, and scripts used to generate the reported treasury-risk results are available in the project repository.[1]

### 5.3 Economic Scalability and Industrial Thresholds

While the 50,000-bid baseline successfully demonstrates the relative risk reduction of the DCA policy, its nominal OPEX ($18.00) is too small to justify the administrative overhead of a complex treasury operation. To evaluate the practical business value of the CPWI architecture for large-scale Auction Organizers (AOs), we conducted a scenario analysis scaling the operational volume to regional (500,000 bids) and national (5,000,000 bids) levels.

As shown in Table 3, while the relative overrun probability remains invariant due to the proportional nature of geometric Brownian motion, the absolute monetary value protected by the treasury policy scales significantly. At a national scale of 5 million bids per year, the baseline OPEX increases to $1,800.00. Under severe market stress (99% VaR), an unhedged spot-purchasing strategy exposes the AO to a 1% probability of cost overruns exceeding $8,484.47. Implementing

[1] https://github.com/tuanle-max/CPWI-B2G-OPEX-Simulation.

**Table 3.** Treasury OPEX Risk Analysis Across Operational Scales (Base Price: $0.12, Fee: 0.003 ALGO)

| Scale (Bids/Year) | Nominal OPEX | 99% Spot VaR | 99% DCA VaR | Absolute Risk Reduction |
|---|---|---|---|---|
| Small (50,000) | $18.00 | $84.84 | $21.21 | $63.63 |
| Regional (500,000) | $180.00 | $848.45 | $212.11 | $636.34 |
| National (5,000,000) | $1,800.00 | $8,484.47 | $2,121.12 | $6,363.35 |

the DCA and 50% reserve policy compresses this extreme tail risk to $2,121.12, yielding an absolute risk reduction of $6,363.35.

Furthermore, if the protocol fee structure incorporates additional on-chain compliance operations (e.g., ASA minting, final asset transfers, or document hashing), this baseline OPEX - and the corresponding absolute savings - would multiply. These results confirm that while fee determinism is a technical prerequisite, the CPWI treasury model delivers its primary industrial value in high-volume, national-scale deployments where absolute financial exposure is substantial enough to warrant treasury management. However, this linear financial scaling does not capture secondary technical non-linearities. At 5 million bids per year, state bloat, Algorand's Minimum Balance Requirements (MBR) for managing thousands of concurrent asset accounts, and archival node storage costs become non-negligible constraints that an AO must factor into the total infrastructure overhead.

## 6 Discussion and Limitations

The CPWI architecture shifts the AO's operational risk from unpredictable network congestion to a manageable exchange-rate planning problem [4]. By anchoring token demand to expected volume, AOs avoid large contingency margins [7], supporting the commercial plausibility of Web3 in fixed-price B2G contracts [1]. Furthermore, constant protocol fees ensure market integrity by preventing bidders from buying priority during high-contention windows [5,17].

However, several limitations exist. Empirically, the 87.00% rejection rate on MainNet indicates direct on-chain submission is unsuitable for high-concurrency auctions. Achieving production-grade B2G SLAs mandates an off-chain sequencing layer to pre-validate and batch bids before on-chain settlement [13,18].

Financially, our analysis assumes specific parameters. As demonstrated in our sensitivity analysis, the DCA protective effect diminishes under severe token depreciation and fails entirely in a token collapse scenario. Moreover, Net OPEX accounting assumes unused reserve tokens retain market value, treating them as balance-sheet assets rather than sunk costs.

Finally, this case study does not model broader implementation overheads (e.g., minimum balance requirements, compliance overhead, node storage). Future work should evaluate integrated end-to-end setups, including asset transfer (ASA) paths, across various deterministic-fee or fee-sponsoring networks to fully capture the total cost of ownership.

## 7 Conclusion

This paper has presented an industry case study of cost-predictable Web3 infrastructure for public asset auctions, reframing OPEX predictability as a first-class deployment requirement for B2G services. Our evidence from Algorand MainNet demonstrates that a deterministic-fee architecture can maintain a constant per-bid cost of 0.003 ALGO and stable latency (median TTF 7.49 s) even under severe bid-sniping workloads. When paired with a DCA-based treasury policy and a 50% reserve, this approach compresses the 99% Cost Overrun VaR by 75%, effectively bridging the gap between volatile infrastructure costs and fixed-price service contracts.

A broader lesson from our scalability analysis is that while fee determinism is a technical prerequisite, the primary industrial value of the CPWI framework emerges at regional and national scales. At high operational volumes (e.g., 5 million bids), the absolute risk reduction provided by treasury management becomes substantial enough to justify the associated administrative overhead. While not a universal solution for all blockchain cost challenges, the integrated design of deterministic execution, hybrid compliance, and rule-based treasury management offers a credible path for the commercial adoption of Web3 in regulated public-sector delivery.

**Acknowledgments.** This study was partially supported by the Lac Viet Auction Partnership Company, KOET Co., Ltd., and Hanoi Open University in Vietnam. The authors gratefully acknowledge the partial financial support and mentorship provided by the Algorand Foundation's Web3 Masterclasses.

## References

1. Akaba, T.I., Norta, A., Udokwu, C., Draheim, D.: A framework for the adoption of blockchain-based e-procurement systems in the public sector. In: Hattingh, M., Matthee, M., Smuts, H., Pappas, I., Dwivedi, Y.K., Mäntymäki, M. (eds.) I3E 2020. LNCS, vol. 12066, pp. 3–14. Springer, Cham (2020). https://doi.org/10.1007/978-3-030-44999-5_1
2. Baranwal, P.R.: Blockchain based full privacy preserving public procurement. In: Chen, Z., Cui, L., Palanisamy, B., Zhang, L.-J. (eds.) ICBC 2020. LNCS, vol. 12404, pp. 3–17. Springer, Cham (2020). https://doi.org/10.1007/978-3-030-59638-5_1
3. Abdelsalam, M., Abouahmed, A., Shatat, A., Hashish, A., AlQodsi, E.: Blockchain and smart public procurement contracts: a comparative legal analysis of digital transformation in the public sector. Access Justice Eastern Europe **8**(4), 242–274 (2025). https://doi.org/10.33327/AJEE-18-8.4-a000137
4. Le, M.T., Nguyen, X.H., Tran, Q.H., Pham, D.K., Do, T.H.: Decentralized auction system for tangible assets and its application. LNCS, vol. 16049. Springer, Cham (2026). https://doi.org/10.1007/978-3-032-02225-7_14
5. Shi, Z., de Laat, C., Grosso, P., Zhao, Z.: Integration of blockchain and auction models: a survey, some applications, and challenges. IEEE Commun. Surv. Tutor. **25**(1), 497–537 (2023). https://doi.org/10.1109/COMST.2022.3222403

6. Chiquito, E., Bodin, U., Schelén, O.: Survey on decentralized auctioning systems. IEEE Access **11**, 51672–51688 (2023). https://doi.org/10.1109/ACCESS.2023.3279914
7. Roughgarden, T.: Transaction fee mechanism design. In: Proceedings of the 22nd ACM Conference on Economics and Computation (EC 2021), p. 792. Association for Computing Machinery, New York (2021). https://doi.org/10.1145/3465456.3467591
8. Reijsbergen, D., Sridhar, S., Monnot, B., Leonardos, S., Skoulakis, S., Piliouras, G.: Transaction fees on a honeymoon: Ethereum's EIP-1559 one month later. In: 2021 IEEE International Conference on Blockchain (Blockchain), pp. 196–204 (2021). https://doi.org/10.1109/Blockchain53845.2021.00034
9. Liu, Y., Lu, Y., Nayak, K., Zhang, F., Zhang, L., Zhao, Y.: Empirical analysis of EIP-1559: transaction fees, waiting times, and consensus security. In: Proceedings of the 2022 ACM SIGSAC Conference on Computer and Communications Security (CCS 2022), pp. 2099–2113. Association for Computing Machinery, New York (2022). https://doi.org/10.1145/3548606.3559341
10. Shi, X.: The role of crypto assets in the traditional banking system and its impact on financial stability. Adv. Econ. Manage. Polit. Sci. **165**, 121–127 (2025). https://doi.org/10.54254/2754-1169/2025.21598
11. Wen, H.: How digital asset treasury companies can survive bear markets: the case of the strategy and bitcoin. arXiv preprint arXiv:2511.01135 (2025). https://doi.org/10.48550/arXiv.2511.01135
12. Bergen, J.: Liquidity management: navigating volatility, regulation, and technological change. J. Payments Strategy Syst. **20**(1) (2026). https://doi.org/10.69554/TBEN5696
13. Tortola, D., Pelosi, A., Di Biase, A., Ricci, L.: Developing payment channels on the Algorand blockchain. In: 2024 6th Conference on Blockchain Research & Applications for Innovative Networks and Services (BRAINS), Berlin, Germany, pp. 1–4 (2024). https://doi.org/10.1109/BRAINS63024.2024.10732211
14. Jotaki, H., Liu, M., Takahashi, H.: A study of the impact of crypto assets on portfolio risk management (2019–2022). J. Interdisc. Econ. **0**(0) (2024). https://doi.org/10.1177/02601079241264878
15. Shahrour, M.H., Lemand, R., Mourey, M.: Cross-market volatility dynamics in crypto and traditional financial instruments: quantifying the spillover effect. J. Risk Finance **26**(1), 1–21 (2025). https://doi.org/10.1108/JRF-07-2024-0185
16. Al Hemairy, M., Abu Talib, M., Khalil, A., et al.: Blockchain-based framework and platform for validation, authentication & equivalency of academic certification and institution's accreditation: UAE case study and system performance. Educ. Inf. Technol. **29**, 18203–18232 (2024). https://doi.org/10.1007/s10639-024-12493-6
17. Rahat, Y.O., Islam, M.K., Rabbani, S.F.: Quantitative and data-driven evaluation of blockchain-based financial systems: transaction efficiency, transparency, cost optimization, and performance metrics in global markets. J. Bus. Manage. Stud. **7**(4), 389–406 (2025). https://doi.org/10.32996/jbms.2025.7.4.20.27
18. Abbasihafshejani, M., Manshaei, M.H., Jadliwala, M.: Detecting and punishing selfish behavior during gossiping in Algorand blockchain. In: 2023 IEEE Virtual Conference on Communications (VCC), NY, USA, pp. 49–55 (2023). https://doi.org/10.1109/VCC60689.2023.10474784

# Blockchain-Based Credential Systems in Higher Education: A Comparative Review and Research Gap Analysis

Driss Echouikhi(✉) and Asmaâ Retbi

RIME Team-Networking, Modeling and e-Learning, Mohammadia School of Engineers (EMI), Mohammed V University, Rabat, Morocco

driss.echouikhi@um5r.ac.ma, retbi@emi.ac.ma

**Abstract.** Blockchain technology has emerged as a transformative infrastructure for securing, verifying, and sharing academic credentials. Over the past nine years (2017–2026), numerous blockchain-based credential systems have been proposed, spanning on-chain platforms, hybrid storage architectures, Self-Sovereign Identity frameworks, and privacy-preserving verification mechanisms. Despite this proliferation, the field remains fragmented: systems are developed in isolation, rarely comply with international standards, and do not integrate with the Learning Management Systems (LMS) in which academic activities are actually conducted. This paper presents a structured comparative review of twenty-four representative blockchain-based credential systems published between 2017 and 2026, identified through searches of major academic databases (IEEE Xplore, ACM Digital Library, Scopus, ScienceDirect, MDPI, and arXiv) and backward snowballing. Each system is analyzed using an author-defined five-criteria framework: blockchain utilization (CR1), smart contract support (CR2), W3C Verifiable Credentials compliance (CR3), LMS integration (CR4), and middleware/interoperability capability (CR5). The review classifies the systems into seven taxonomic categories across five evolutionary phases, and derives six research gaps from the comparative matrix. The key finding is that no analyzed system satisfies all five criteria simultaneously: while blockchain utilization is near-universal, W3C compliance, LMS integration, and middleware interoperability remain critically underexplored. The complete absence of university-level middleware architectures connecting LMS platforms to blockchain-based credential infrastructure via full W3C standards constitutes the most significant gap. A six-direction research agenda is proposed to guide future work.

**Keywords:** Blockchain · Academic Credentials · Comparative Review · Verifiable Credentials · Learning Management Systems · Decentralized Identifiers · Research Gap Analysis · Middleware · Interoperability


H. Huang et al. (Eds.): ICBC 2026, LNCS 16959, pp. 83–97, 2027.
https://doi.org/10.1007/978-3-032-36766-2_6

# 1 Introduction

The integrity of academic credentials is a cornerstone of the global education and employment ecosystem, yet verification remains largely manual, centralized, and fraud-prone. Academic fraud is estimated at ~ $21 billion, with diploma mills generating ~ $7 billion annually [1, 2]; cases such as the Axact network (215,000 fake credentials across 197 countries [3]) and Operation Nightingale (7,600 + fraudulent nursing diplomas [4]) show this is a systemic crisis.

Meanwhile, digitization—accelerated by COVID-19, which affected 220M + tertiary students [5]—has made LMS platforms, especially Moodle (507M + users, 146,683 sites, 235 countries [6]), the backbone of digital education. Yet most LMS-generated credentials lack interoperability and tamper-evident verification: a degree from Mohammed V University cannot be programmatically verified abroad without bilateral arrangements, impeding the learner mobility central to the Bologna Process.

Blockchain offers immutability, transparency, decentralization, and cryptographic verifiability [7], making it a natural fit for credential integrity. Since Blockcerts (MIT, 2016) [8], numerous systems have appeared, propelled by the W3C VC Data Model 2.0 [9], DIDs v1.0 [10], Layer-2 scaling (~$0.002–0.01/credential [11, 22]), EBSI (40 + nodes, 29 countries [12]), and eIDAS 2.0 mandating EUDI Wallets by December 2026 [13].

Several prior reviews exist: Rustemi et al. [14] (34 systems, 2018–2022), Alsobhi et al. [15] (15 micro-credentialing systems), Silaghi and Popescu [16], Alammary et al. [17] (2016–2019), and Loukil et al. [18]. They share three limitations: none covers the transformative 2023–2026 period (W3C VC 2.0, zk-SNARK verification, Layer-2, eIDAS 2.0); none evaluates LMS integration or middleware/interoperability as explicit criteria; and none synthesizes findings into formally justified, quantitatively supported gaps.

This paper addresses these limitations through a structured comparative review of twenty-four representative blockchain-based credential systems (2017–2026), analyzed against an explicit five-criteria evaluation framework.

The contributions are as follows:

**C1:** A comprehensive comparative review of 24 blockchain-based credential systems (2017–2026), based on a transparent analysis across six academic databases, extending coverage to the critical 2023–2026 period not addressed by prior reviews.

**C2:** A five-criteria evaluation framework (CR1–CR5) that, for the first time, incorporates LMS integration and middleware/interoperability capability as explicit assessment dimensions, alongside blockchain utilization, smart contract support, and W3C Verifiable Credentials compliance.

**C3:** A seven-category taxonomic classification spanning five evolutionary phases (2016–2026), accompanied by quality assessment scoring for each primary study.

**C4:** The identification and formal justification of six research gaps supported by quantitative evidence from the CR1–CR5 matrix, culminating in a six-direction research agenda.

**C5:** A comparative analysis with six prior systematic reviews, demonstrating the novel coverage and analytical depth of this review.

# 2 Background

## 2.1 Blockchain Technology and Smart Contracts

Blockchain [20] is a distributed ledger maintaining a tamper-evident chain of blocks across a peer-to-peer network. Ethereum [21, 22] added Turing-complete smart contracts that automate issuance, revocation, and verification logic without intermediaries. Ethereum Layer-1 costs ($0.20–5 per operation, ~ 12 s block time [11]) have motivated Layer-2 solutions: Polygon PoS [23] reaches ~ 7,200 TPS at $0.002–0.01 per transaction, while zk-rollups (zkSync [49], Arbitrum, Optimism) inherit Ethereum security while reducing costs by 90–99%.

## 2.2 W3C Verifiable Credentials and Decentralized Identifiers

The W3C Verifiable Credentials Data Model 2.0 [9] (W3C Recommendation, 15 May 2025) standardizes cryptographically verifiable attestations comprising context, type, credential subject, issuer, validity, and proof. The companion Decentralized Identifiers (DIDs) v1.0 [10] enable Self-Sovereign Identity through user-controlled identifiers resolved to DID Documents. Together they form a trust triangle (issuer–holder–verifier); the Bitstring Status List [9] provides efficient revocation.

## 2.3 Learning Management Systems and the LMS-Credential Gap

LMS platforms are the operational backbone of digital higher education; Moodle (146,683 sites, 235 countries [6]) is widely deployed across Moroccan universities [11, 24]. Despite generating rich academic data, LMS lack any native capability to issue blockchain-based or W3C-compliant credentials—the gap between where academic events occur (the LMS) and where credentials could be anchored (the blockchain) is the central challenge motivating this review.

## 2.4 European and Moroccan Institutional Context

EBSI [12] (40 + nodes, 29 countries) and the EDC framework (76,000 + credentials [25]) anchor the European context; eIDAS 2.0 [13] mandates EUDI Wallets by December 2026. In Morocco, 12 universities serve 1.25M + students at low IT maturity (COBIT 5 level 2/5) [11]; contributions include BlockMEDC [11], SmartDegrees at Hassan II University [26], and the legal analyses of Litoussi et al. [27] and Taqiddine and Aziz [28], the legal framework not yet covering distributed ledgers.

# 3 Research Methodology

This paper presents a structured comparative review of blockchain-based academic credential systems. Sources, selection rationale, evaluation criteria, and analysis instruments are explicitly documented to ensure transparency and partial replication, without claiming to follow a registered systematic-review protocol.

### 3.1 Research Questions

**RQ1:** What blockchain-based academic credential systems have been proposed between 2017 and 2026, and what are their technical characteristics in terms of blockchain platform, identity model, credential standard, storage strategy, privacy mechanism, and deployment maturity?

**RQ2:** To what extent do existing systems satisfy five evaluation criteria: blockchain utilization (CR1), smart contract support (CR2), W3C Verifiable Credentials compliance (CR3), LMS integration (CR4), and middleware/interoperability capability (CR5)?

**RQ3:** How has the field evolved chronologically, and what thematic categories characterize the research landscape?

**RQ4:** What research gaps exist at the intersection of blockchain technology, LMS platforms, and verifiable credential standards, and what directions should future research pursue?

### 3.2 Search Strategy

Relevant work was identified through six academic sources—IEEE Xplore, ACM Digital Library, Scopus, ScienceDirect/Elsevier, MDPI, and arXiv—selected for their coverage of blockchain and educational technology research. The query, adapted per source syntax, was:

*("blockchain" OR "distributed ledger" OR "smart contract" OR "DLT") AND ("credential" OR "certificate" OR "diploma" OR "degree" OR "academic record" OR "micro-credential") AND ("education" OR "higher education" OR "university" OR "e-learning" OR "LMS" OR "learning management").*

Searches covered January 2017 – March 2026. Backward snowballing was applied to the references of selected systems and prior reviews to find work not surfaced by the database searches.

Inclusion criteria: (I1) Peer-reviewed journal articles, conference papers, or preprints proposing, implementing, or evaluating a blockchain-based system for academic credential management; (I2) Published between January 2017 and March 2026; (I3) Written in English; (I4) Providing sufficient technical detail to assess at least three of the five evaluation criteria (CR1–CR5).

Exclusion criteria: (E1) Literature reviews, secondary studies, or opinion papers with no system contribution; (E2) Studies exclusively addressing non-academic credentials (healthcare, supply chain, professional certifications); (E3) Duplicate publications of the same system—the most complete or most recent version was retained; (E4) Studies shorter than 4 pages or lacking technical substance; (E5) Systems addressing only assessment or examination management without credential issuance.

### 3.3 Study Selection Process

Studies were retained when they (I1) proposed, implemented, or evaluated a blockchain-based system for academic credential management; (I2) were published between January 2017 and March 2026; (I3) in English; and (I4) provided enough detail to assess at least three of the five criteria. Excluded: pure secondary or opinion pieces, non-academic credentials, duplicate reports of an already-included system, and studies lacking technical substance.

From the identified literature, twenty-four systems were retained for in-depth analysis: the most representative of the field's technical diversity, sufficiently documented for the five criteria, and collectively spanning 2017–2026 and the main architectural families.

### 3.4 Data Extraction and Quality Assessment

For each of the twenty-four systems, a standardized form captured: name, authors, year, venue, country, blockchain platform, consensus, credential format, identity model, storage, privacy mechanism, revocation, LMS integration, interoperability, deployment maturity, and CR1–CR5 (Yes/No/Partial). System maturity was appraised qualitatively (architectural detail, prototype, evaluation, comparison with prior work).

### 3.5 Analysis Framework

Systems were analyzed with three instruments: a ten-dimension comparison matrix; the author-defined CR1–CR5 framework; and a seven-category taxonomy from iterative coding (T1 standalone platforms, T2 LMS-integrated, T3 hybrid storage, T4 privacy-preserving, T5 interoperability/middleware, T6 standards/governance, T7 regional). A temporal analysis identifies five evolutionary phases. CR1–CR5 were derived from W3C VC/DID specifications and a deployment-oriented perspective; ratings were assigned from the technical evidence reported in each primary source according to explicit rubrics. A criterion is rated Yes when the system fully implements the capability, Partial when it implements it incompletely or for a subset of cases, and No when the capability is absent. Specifically, CR1 (blockchain) is Yes when records are anchored on-chain; CR2 (smart contracts) is Yes when issuance, verification, or revocation logic runs in deployed contracts and Partial when contracts are only proposed; CR3 (W3C VC) is Yes when the system implements the W3C Verifiable Credentials Data Model, Partial when it uses DIDs or JSON-LD without full conformance, and No when no W3C standard is used; CR4 (LMS integration) is Yes when the system issues or verifies credentials from within an LMS and Partial when integration is limited or prototypal; and CR5 (middleware/interoperability) is Yes when a reusable abstraction layer connects an LMS to the blockchain and Partial when only cross-system exchange or partial interoperability is supported.

## 4 Results

### 4.1 Overview and Temporal Distribution (RQ3)

The 24 primary systems span five evolutionary phases:

**Phase 1 (2016–2017)**—Pioneers: Blockcerts [8] demonstrated the feasibility of credentials anchored on the Bitcoin blockchain with 111 MIT graduates, establishing the proof of concept.

**Phase 2 (2018–2019)**—Early platforms: EduCTX [29] introduced ECTS credit tokenization on the Ark blockchain platform (IEEE Access, 500 + citations); UniChain [30] proposed permissioned access control; Karataş [31] developed a Moodle-Ethereum integration for document verification; Shen and Xiao [32] proposed a dual-layer consortium blockchain for online quiz assessment.

**Phase 3 (2020–2021)**—Expansion: EduChain [33] introduced a heterogeneous dual-blockchain architecture; IU-SmartCert [34] implemented selective disclosure via Merkle trees; E-Learning Chain [35] applied distributed ledger technology to e-learning certification.

**Phase 4 (2022–2023)**—Standards emergence: Digital Brick [36] achieved LMS integration via SCORM with Open Badges; ELMO2EDS [37] bridged the EMREX academic exchange network and the SSI ecosystem via EBSI; Scorechain [38] was built on Substrate/Polkadot; the EBSI/EDC framework [12] achieved W3C Verifiable Credentials compliance at the European scale.

**Phase 5 (2024–2026)**—Maturity: BACIP [39] and ZKBAR-V [19] introduced Zero-Knowledge Proof-based privacy; BlockMEDC [11] deployed an Ethereum Layer-2 solution for Morocco; QualiChain [40, 48] combined Hyperledger Iroha and the SSI paradigm for lifelong learning in the European Union, with W3C Verifiable Credentials integration planned as future work; PublicEduChain [41] proposed learner-owned data on a public blockchain; ShikkhaChain [42] targeted Bangladesh; CredChain [43] implemented academic and professional credential verification; BlockAdemiC [44] piloted a multi-chain SSI system in Greece; Tanim et al. [50] proposed in 2026 a decentralized framework for stackable academic microcredentials on Hyperledger Besu (QBFT, IPFS), implementing a full credential lifecycle through Solidity smart contracts and evaluated via Hyperledger Caliper (1.6–2.0 TPS, 1.88 s latency)—one of the most rigorous contributions of the 2024–2026 period.

Publication venues reflect the field's multidisciplinary nature: IEEE Access (4), IEEE conferences (3), MDPI journals (4), Springer CCIS/LNCS (3), ACM DLT (1), arXiv (3), and specialized journals (5), spanning 16 countries led by Europe (7), Asia (6), MENA (5), the Americas (3), and Oceania (3).

### 4.2 Five-Criteria Comparative Analysis (RQ1, RQ2)

Table 1 presents the complete CR1–CR5 evaluation of the 24 primary systems, the analysis reveals marked asymmetries across the five dimensions.

**Aggregate statistics reveal an inverted pattern. CR1 (blockchain): 23/24 (96%)—near-universal. CR2 (smart contracts): 17/24 full + 3 partial (71%). CR3 (W3C VC): only 2/24 full (8%) + 6 partial—severely deficient (full only in EBSI/EDC** [12] **and ELMO2EDS** [37]**). CR4 (LMS integration): 4/24 full + 1 partial (17%). CR5 (middleware/interoperability): 0/24 full, 5/24 partial (21%). The field has mastered blockchain fundamentals but systematically neglected standards compliance, LMS connectivity, and interoperability—the dimensions most critical for deployment.**

Detailed analysis confirms the asymmetry. Standalone platforms dominate (13 systems: Blockcerts [8], EduCTX [29], UniChain [30], ShikkhaChain [42], CredChain [43],

PublicEduChain [41], BlockMEDC [11], Tanim et al. [50]) but most lack W3C compliance and LMS connection. Only four systems integrate an LMS—Karataş [31], Digital Brick [36], E-Learning Chain [35], PublicEduChain [41]—none in full W3C form; John and Hürten [45] extend Moodle badges without blockchain. EBSI/EDC [12] and ELMO2EDS [37] reach the most advanced W3C compliance but operate at registry or inter-institutional level, not LMS. ZKBAR-V [19], BACIP [39], and IU-SmartCert [34] lead privacy (ZKP, selective disclosure) but none connects to an LMS. Among standalone platforms, BlockMEDC [11] is one of the more architecturally detailed (Ethereum Layer-2, IPFS) but, like the others, implements neither W3C Verifiable Credentials nor LMS integration; it is treated here with the same analytical distance as the remaining systems. Indexed-journal systems generally report more complete architectures and evaluations than short conference papers or preprints, which mostly remain proof-of-concept. A further qualification concerns industrial platforms excluded from the corpus for lack of peer-reviewed publications. Widely deployed services such as Credly, Accredible, and BCDiploma offer mature credential management and, in several cases, native LMS connectors (Credly provides Canvas and Moodle plugins) and verification middleware. Their existence nuances the CR5 = 0/24 finding for the academic literature: practical LMS-oriented middleware exists commercially, but remains largely proprietary and undocumented in scholarly venues, and generally does not implement the full W3C Verifiable Credentials stack required for cross-border interoperability.

Table 2 compares this review with six prior secondary studies to demonstrate its added value.

**Table 1.** Five-criteria evaluation of 24 blockchain-based credential systems (2017–2026).Y: Yes; N: No; P: Partial.

| # | System [Ref] | CR1 | CR2 | CR3 | CR4 | CR5 | Year / Country |
|---|---|---|---|---|---|---|---|
| 1 | Blockcerts [8] | Y | N | N | N | N | 2016 / USA |
| 2 | EduCTX [29] | Y | P | N | N | N | 2018 / Slovenia |
| 3 | Shen & Xiao [32] | Y | Y | N | N | N | 2018 / China |
| 4 | Karataş [31] | Y | Y | N | Y | N | 2018 / Turkey |
| 5 | UniChain [30] | Y | Y | N | N | N | 2019 / Palestine |
| 6 | SmartDegrees [26] | Y | Y | P | N | N | 2019 / Spain-Morocco |
| 7 | E-Learning Chain [35] | Y | P | N | P | N | 2020 / Saudi Arabia |
| 8 | EduChain [33] | Y | Y | N | N | N | 2021 / China |

(*continued*)

**Table 1.** (*continued*)

| # | System [Ref] | CR1 | CR2 | CR3 | CR4 | CR5 | Year / Country |
|---|---|---|---|---|---|---|---|
| 9 | IU-SmartCert [34] | Y | Y | N | N | N | 2021 / Vietnam |
| 10 | Digital Brick [36] | Y | N | N | Y | N | 2022 / Italy |
| 11 | ELMO2EDS [37] | Y | N | Y | N | P | 2022 / Germany |
| 12 | Litoussi et al [27] | Y | P | N | N | N | 2022 / Morocco |
| 13 | Scorechain [38] | Y | Y | N | N | N | 2023 / Japan-Vietnam |
| 14 | EBSI/EDC [12] | Y | Y | Y | N | P | 2023 / EU (29) |
| 15 | PublicEduChain [41] | Y | Y | N | Y | N | 2024 / Turkey |
| 16 | CredChain [43] | Y | Y | N | N | N | 2024 / Bangladesh |
| 17 | BACIP [39] | Y | Y | P | N | P | 2024 / Australia |
| 18 | QualiChain [40] | Y | Y | P | N | P | 2024 / EU |
| 19 | BlockMEDC [11] | Y | Y | N | N | N | 2025 / Morocco |
| 20 | ZKBAR-V [19] | Y | Y | P | N | N | 2025 / NZ-AU |
| 21 | ShikkhaChain [42] | Y | Y | N | N | N | 2025 / Bangladesh |
| 22 | BlockAdemiC [44] | Y | Y | P | N | N | 2025 / Greece |
| 23 | John & Hürten [45] | N | N | P | Y | N | 2025 / Germany |
| 24 | Tanim et al [50] | Y | Y | N | N | P | 2026 / Bangladesh Malaysia |

CR1: Blockchain, CR2: Smart Contracts, CR3: W3C VC Compliance, CR4: LMS Integration, CR5: Middleware/Interoperability.

**Table 2.** Comparison with prior reviews. This review is the first to include CR3 (W3C VC), CR4 (LMS), and CR5 (Middleware) as explicit evaluation criteria and to derive six formally justified research gaps from a comparative matrix. Y: Yes; N: No; P: Partial.

| Review | Period | Syst. | CR3 VC | CR4 LMS | CR5 Midlew | Gaps | Review |
|---|---|---|---|---|---|---|---|
| Rustemi [14] | 2018–2022 | 34 | N | N | N | P | N |
| Alsobhi [15] | 2016–2022 | 15 | N | N | N | P | N |
| Silaghi [16] | 2017–2024 | 18 | N | N | N | Y | N |
| Alammary [17] | 2016–2019 | 28 | N | N | N | N | Y |
| Loukil [18] | 2016–2020 | — | N | N | N | P | N |
| Grech [7] | 2017 | — | N | N | N | N | N |
| This review | 2017–2026 | 24 | Y | Y | Y | Y(6) | Y |

## 5 Research Gap Analysis (RQ4)

The CR1–CR5 matrix, taxonomic classification, and quality assessment reveal six formally justified research gaps. For each gap, quantitative data from the evaluation matrix are provided, along with an analysis of the most relevant existing work and unresolved challenges.

**Gap 1—Absence of Middleware Between LMS and Blockchain:** No university-level system provides full middleware (CR5 = 0/24); only five achieve partial interoperability. Systems either replace the LMS with a native blockchain platform or remain standalone and disconnected from LMS infrastructure. ELMO2EDS [37] bridges the EMREX network rather than LMS platforms; QualiChain [40] targets institutional registries. The middleware approach—abstracting LMS heterogeneity through API adapters without modifying source code—remains unexplored in higher education.

**Gap 2—Absence of the Triple Combination: LMS + Blockchain + W3C:** The intersection of LMS integration (4/24), blockchain (23/24), and W3C VC compliance (2/24) is virtually empty: Digital Brick [36] connects to the LMS but uses Open Badges; EBSI [12] is W3C-compliant but has no LMS link; Karataş [31] connects Moodle without any credential standard. No system integrates all three concurrently in higher education—a critical absence since operational deployment requires all three.

**Gap 3—LMS Integration Without W3C Standards:** Among the four LMS-integrated systems, none implements W3C VCs in full: Digital Brick [36] uses Open Badges (incompatible with EBSI and EUDI Wallets); Karataş [31] uses raw Ethereum transactions; E-Learning Chain [35] and PublicEduChain [41] lack standards compliance; John and Hürten [45] extend Moodle badges without blockchain. Existing LMS-integrated systems therefore cannot join the emerging European digital credential infrastructure.

**Gap 4—EBSI/EDC Without LMS Connection:** EBSI [12] and the EDC framework (76,000 + credentials [25]) operate at national-registry level: credentials are issued through institutional portals, not LMS interfaces, as illustrated by the Belgium–Italy cross-border pilot [46]. A teacher using Moodle cannot issue an EBSI-compliant VC from their teaching environment; the LMS–EBSI middleware layer does not exist.

**Gap 5—Privacy Mechanisms Disconnected from LMS:** ZKBAR-V [19], BACIP [39], and IU-SmartCert [34] represent the privacy frontier (Zero-Knowledge Proofs, selective disclosure), but none connects to an LMS or implements the full W3C VC 2.0 selective-disclosure framework. How to trigger ZKP-embedded credential issuance from a Moodle environment remains unanswered.

**Gap 6—Regional Deployments Without Middleware Solutions:** Despite regional contributions—BlockMEDC [11] (Morocco), ShikkhaChain [42]/CredChain [43] (Bangladesh), QualiChain [40]/BlockAdemiC [44] (EU)—no regional implementation provides middleware connecting national LMS infrastructure to the blockchain via W3C standards. The Moroccan context (12 universities on Moodle, 1.25M students, COBIT 5 maturity 2/5 [11]) requires incremental-adoption middleware rather than disruptive platform replacement.

## 6 Discussion and Research Agenda

### 6.1 Key Findings

Four major findings emerge from this review:

First, the field shows a striking asymmetry between infrastructure maturity and deployment readiness: blockchain (96%) and smart-contract support (71%) are well established, but W3C compliance (8%), LMS integration (17%), and middleware (0% full)—the dimensions determining usability—remain underdeveloped, explaining the persistent prototype-to-production gap.

Second, the field evolved through five phases (proof of concept → platform construction → expansion → standards emergence → maturity), but additively rather than integratively: each phase added capabilities without connecting them to the LMS infrastructure universities actually use.

Third, three communities—LMS developers, blockchain engineers, and standards bodies—operate in silos: LMS research produces Moodle plugins without blockchain, blockchain research produces platforms without LMS support, and standards work produces VC/DID specifications without LMS integration. The absence of full university-level middleware (CR5 = 0/24) is a direct consequence.

Fourth, beyond technical factors, data-protection law is a decisive constraint on LMS integration that the analyzed systems largely overlook. In the United States, FERPA governs the privacy of student education records, while in the European Union the GDPR restricts the processing of personal data and grants rights such as erasure that are difficult to reconcile with an immutable ledger. These regimes discourage storing personal or identifying data on-chain and favour architectures that anchor only cryptographic commitments while keeping personal data off-chain under user control. Compliance therefore reinforces, rather than relaxes, the case for a privacy-preserving middleware layer that mediates between the LMS and the blockchain, and it helps explain why direct on-chain integration with mainstream LMS platforms has not been adopted in practice.

### 6.2 Research Agenda

Based on the six identified gaps, the following research agenda is proposed, ordered by priority and feasibility:

**RA1**—Middleware architectures for LMS–blockchain integration (Gaps 1–3): the most critical need—middleware that intercepts LMS events via API adapters (Adapter pattern [47]) and generates W3C-compliant VCs anchored on the blockchain without modifying LMS source code, supporting Moodle, Canvas, and LTI through a unified interface.

Milestone: a minimum viable middleware—a Moodle plugin issuing W3C VCs to a Layer-2 testnet.

**RA2**—Standards integration and EBSI connectivity (Gaps 2, 4): adopt W3C VC 2.0 [9] and DIDs [10] as the universal interoperability layer, with native EBSI [12]/EUDI Wallet [13] compatibility and Bitstring Status List revocation.

Milestone: a credential that passes EBSI conformance testing and verifies in a reference EUDI wallet.

**RA3**—Privacy-by-design (Gap 5): integrate zk-SNARKs and BBS + signatures into the issuance pipeline (not as standalone tools), with selective disclosure compliant with GDPR Article 5(1)(c) and equivalent national laws [28].

Milestone: selective disclosure of a single attribute (e.g., degree class) without revealing the full credential, verified on-chain.

**RA4**—Economic viability at university scale (Gaps 1, 6): systematically benchmark Layer-2 solutions (~\$0.01/credential [11]) for deployments above 1M students; cost models must include infrastructure, gas, IPFS pinning, and maintenance.

Milestone: a verified per-credential cost below \$0.01 at a simulated load of 1M credentials.

**RA5**—Credential lifecycle management (Gap 2): formal lifecycle (issuance, active use, suspension, revocation, renewal, expiration, archival) with defined state transitions and invariants—absent from current literature.

Milestone: a formal state machine over all seven lifecycle states, with revocation verifiable within one block.

**RA6**—Regional contextualization and deployment studies (Gap 6): solutions must account for legal frameworks, LMS preferences, infrastructure maturity, and change management, validated through longitudinal deployment studies with real institutional partners. Milestone: a pilot at one Moroccan university issuing verifiable diplomas to a real graduating cohort over one academic year.

## 7 Threats to Validity

**Construct Validity:** The CR1–CR5 framework was developed by the authors and derived from established W3C specifications and the deployment-oriented perspective of this review; alternative frameworks could yield different gap configurations. The novel criteria CR4 and CR5 distinguish this review from prior ones.

**Internal Validity:** This review is comparative rather than exhaustive. The selection of twenty-four systems prioritizes representativeness and technical depth over completeness, and was performed by the authors without independent double screening. Querying six academic sources supplemented by backward snowballing mitigates coverage bias, but industrial systems lacking academic publications (e.g., BCDiploma, Accredible, Credly) are not captured—these represent a significant body of practical knowledge. The CR1–CR5 ratings involve author judgment, mitigated by relying on the technical evidence reported in each primary source and on established W3C specifications.

**External Validity:** The review focuses on academic credentials in higher education (2017–2026) and may not generalize to professional certifications, K-12, or corporate training. English-language coverage may underrepresent non-Anglophone communities.

**Reliability:** The sources, search query, selection criteria, extraction schema, and analysis framework are documented to support transparency and partial replication. This review is comparative rather than systematic and does not claim to follow a registered protocol; the selection of twenty-four systems prioritizes representativeness and technical depth over exhaustiveness.

## 8 Conclusion

This paper has presented a structured comparative review of blockchain-based academic credential systems covering the period 2017–2026, drawing on searches of six academic sources and backward snowballing. Twenty-four representative systems were analyzed using an author-defined five-criteria evaluation framework (CR1–CR5) assessing blockchain utilization, smart contract support, W3C Verifiable Credentials compliance, LMS integration, and middleware/interoperability capability.

The review yields five key findings: (i) near-universal blockchain adoption (CR1 = 96%) but severe gaps in standards (CR3 = 8%), LMS integration (CR4 = 17%), and middleware (CR5 = 0% full); (ii) five evolutionary phases (2016–2026) added capabilities additively rather than integratively, leaving the LMS–blockchain gap unresolved; (iii) six formally justified research gaps, the most critical being the absence of full middleware connecting LMS to blockchain via W3C standards; (iv) three communities—LMS developers, blockchain engineers, and standards bodies—operate in silos; (v) the 2023–2026 enabling technologies (W3C VC 2.0, Layer-2, ZKP, eIDAS 2.0) make integrated middleware feasible and urgent for the first time.The six-direction research agenda proposed in this paper—middleware architectures, standards integration, privacy-by-design, economic viability, credential lifecycle management, and regional contextualization—provides a roadmap for the next phase of the field's evolution.

While this review focused on LMS platforms, the middleware gap extends equally to MOOC platforms, which generate comparable credential volumes without blockchain integration. Future work will accordingly design, implement, and evaluate a decentralized blockchain-based middleware enabling the automated aggregation, cryptographic certification, and instant verification of credentials from heterogeneous LMS and MOOC platforms, compliant with Self-Sovereign Identity principles and personal data protection. A companion paper detailing the proposed architecture is forthcoming.

## References


1. Ravaioli, S.: Global Financial Impact of Diploma Mills and Academic Fraud, Parchment / Instructure, 30 Sep. (2025). https://www.parchment.com/blog/global-financial-impact-of-diploma-mills-and-academic-fraud/
2. Ezell, A., Bear, J., Mills, D.: The Billion-Dollar Industry That Has Sold Over a Million Fake Diplomas. Prometheus Books (2012)
3. Walsh, D.: Fake Diplomas, Real Cash: Pakistani Company Axact Reaps Millions, The New York Times, 17 May (2015). https://www.nytimes.com/2015/05/18/world/asia/fake-diplomas-real-cash-pakistani-company-axact-reaps-millions-columbiana-barkley.html
4. U.S. Department of Justice, "Fraudulent Nursing Diploma Scheme Leads to Federal Charges Against 25 Defendants, Press Release, 25 Jan (2023). https://www.justice.gov/usao-sdfl/pr/fraudulent-nursing-diploma-scheme-leads-federal-charges-against-25-defendants
5. UNESCO IESALC, COVID-19 and Higher Education: Today and Tomorrow — Impact, Response, and Transformation, 2020. Updated: "COVID-19: Reopening and Reimagining Universities," UNESDOC: ark:/48223/pf0000378174 (2021)
6. Moodle, "Moodle Statistics, stats.moodle.org (2026). https://stats.moodle.org/
7. Grech, A., Camilleri, A.F.: Blockchain in Education, JRC Science for Policy Report, EUR 28778 EN (2017). https://doi.org/10.2760/60649
8. Schmidt, J.P.: Blockcerts — An Open Infrastructure for Academic Credentials on the Blockchain, MIT Media Lab (2016)
9. Sporny, M., et al.: Verifiable Credentials Data Model v2.0, W3C Recommendation, 15 May (2025). https://www.w3.org/TR/vc-data-model-2.0/
10. Sporny, M., et al.: Decentralized Identifiers (DIDs) v1.0, W3C Recommendation, 19 Jul (2022). https://www.w3.org/TR/did-core/
11. Fartitchou, M., Lamaakal, I., El Makkaoui, K., El Allali, Z., Maleh, Y.: BlockMEDC: blockchain smart contracts system for securing moroccan higher education digital certificates. IEEE Access **13**, 39152–39175 (2025). https://doi.org/10.1109/ACCESS.2025.3546177
12. European Commission, European Blockchain Services Infrastructure (EBSI) (2024). https://ec.europa.eu/digital-building-blocks/sites/spaces/EBSI/overview
13. European Parliament, Regulation (EU) 2024/1183 on electronic identification and trust services (eIDAS 2.0), Official Journal of the EU, 30 April (2024). https://eur-lex.europa.eu/legal-content/EN/TXT/?uri=OJ:L_202401183
14. Rustemi, A., Dalipi, F., Atanasovski, B., Risteski, A.: A systematic literature review on blockchain-based systems for academic certificate verification. IEEE Access **11**, 64679–64696 (2023). https://doi.org/10.1109/ACCESS.2023.3289598
15. Alsobhi, H.A., et al.: Blockchain-based micro-credentialing system in higher education institutions: systematic literature review. Knowl.-Based Syst. 265, 110238 (2023). https://doi.org/10.1016/j.knosys.2022.110238
16. Silaghi, G.C., Popescu, D.E.: A systematic review of blockchain-based initiatives in comparison to best practices used in higher education institutions. Computers **14**(4), 141 (2025). https://doi.org/10.3390/computers14040141
17. Alammary, A., Alhazmi, S., Almasri, M., Gillani, S.: Blockchain-based applications in education: a systematic review. Appl. Sci. **9**(12), 2400 (2019). https://doi.org/10.3390/app9122400
18. Loukil, F., Abed, M., Boukadi, K.: Blockchain adoption in education: a systematic literature review. Educ. Inf. Technol. **26**(5), 5779–5797 (2021). https://doi.org/10.1007/s10639-021-10481-8
19. Berrios Moya, J.A., Ayoade, J., Uddin, M.A.: A zero-knowledge proof-enabled blockchain-based academic record verification system. Sensors **25**(11), art. 3450 (2025). https://doi.org/10.3390/s25113450

20. Nakamoto, S.: Bitcoin: A Peer-to-Peer Electronic Cash System (2008). https://bitcoin.org/bitcoin.pdf
21. Buterin, V.: Ethereum: A Next-Generation Smart Contract and Decentralized Application Platform, Ethereum White Paper, 2013 (updated 2024). https://ethereum.org/en/whitepaper/
22. Wood, G.: Ethereum: A Secure Decentralised Generalised Transaction Ledger, Ethereum Yellow Paper 2014 (updated 2024). https://ethereum.github.io/yellowpaper/paper.pdf
23. Polygon Technology, Polygon PoS Documentation (2024). https://docs.polygon.technology/
24. Bouhafs, A.: L'usage de la plateforme Moodle à l'université marocaine. Rev. Int. Technol. Pédag. Univ. **18**(1), 125–138 (2021). https://doi.org/10.18162/ritpu-2021-v18n1-12
25. European Commission, "European Digital Credentials for Learning," Europass (2024). https://europass.europa.eu/en/european-digital-credentials
26. SmartDegrees, "Université Hassan II de Casablanca — Blockchain-Certified Degrees (2019). https://www.smartdegrees.es/
27. Litoussi, M., et al.: Digital certifications in moroccan universities: concepts, challenges, and solutions. Procedia Comput. Sci. **201**, 95–100 (2022). https://doi.org/10.1016/j.procs.2022.03.015
28. Taqiddine, M., Aziz, K. : Réinventer l'archivage numérique marocain à l'ère de la blockchain et des smart contracts. Revue-IRS **3**(3) (2025). https://doi.org/10.5281/zenodo.15516484
29. Turkanović, M., Hölbl, M., Košič, K., Heričko, M., Kamišalić, A.: EduCTX: a blockchain-based higher education credit platform. IEEE Access **6**, 5112–5127 (2018). https://doi.org/10.1109/ACCESS.2018.2789929
30. Daraghmi, E.-Y., Daraghmi, Y.-A., Yuan, S.-M.: UniChain: a design of blockchain-based system for electronic academic records access and permissions management. Appl. Sci. **9**(22), 4966 (2019). https://doi.org/10.3390/app9224966
31. Karataş, E.: Developing ethereum blockchain-based document verification smart contract for moodle learning management system. Bilişim Teknol. Dergisi **11**(4), 399–406 (2018). https://doi.org/10.17671/gazibtd.452686
32. Shen, H., Xiao, Y.: Research on online quiz scheme based on double-layer consortium blockchain. In: Proc. 9th Int. Conf. ITME, pp. 956–960 (2018). https://doi.org/10.1109/ITME.2018.00213
33. Liu, Y., Li, K., Huang, Z., Li, B., Wang, G., Cai, W.: EduChain: a blockchain-based education data management system. CCIS, vol. 1305, pp. 66–81. Springer (2021). https://doi.org/10.1007/978-981-33-6478-3_5
34. Tran, T.-T., Le, H.-D.: IU-SmartCert: a blockchain-based system for academic credentials with selective disclosure. CCIS, vol. 1500, pp. 293–309. Springer (2021). https://doi.org/10.1007/978-981-16-8062-5_20
35. Alruwaili, F.F.: E-learning chain: a secure blockchain approach to e-learning & certification systems. ITJEMAST **11**(16), 1–11 (2020). https://doi.org/10.14456/ITJEMAST.2020.323
36. Mainetti, L., Paiano, R., Pedone, M., Quarta, M., Dervishi, E.: Digital brick: enhancing the student experience using blockchain, open badges and recommendations. Educ. Sci. **12**(8), 567 (2022). https://doi.org/10.3390/educsci12080567
37. Herbke, P., Yildiz, H.: ELMO2EDS: transforming educational credentials into self-sovereign identity paradigm. In: Proc. 20th Int. Conf. ITHET. IEEE (2022). https://doi.org/10.1109/ITHET56107.2022.10031276
38. Tran, V.D., Ata, S., Tran, T.H., Lam, D.K., Pham, H.L.: Blockchain-powered education: a sustainable approach for secured and connected university systems. Sustainability **15**(21), 15545 (2023). https://doi.org/10.3390/su152115545
39. Berrios Moya, J.A.: Blockchain for Academic Integrity: Developing the Blockchain Academic Credential Interoperability Protocol (BACIP), arXiv:2406.15482, (2024)

40. Kontzinos, C., Karakolis, P., Kokkinakos, O, Skalidakis, I., Askounis, A, Psarras, D.: Application and evaluation of a blockchain-centric platform for smart badge accreditation in higher education institutions. Appl. Sci. **14**(12), art. 5191 (2024). https://doi.org/10.3390/app14125191
41. Tanriverdi, M.: PublicEduChain: a framework for sharing student-owned educational data on public blockchain network. IEEE Access **12** (2024). https://doi.org/10.1109/ACCESS.2024.3385660
42. Farabi, A., et al.: ShikkhaChain: A Blockchain-Powered Academic Credential Verification System for Bangladesh, arXiv:2508.05334, (2025)
43. Ahmed, S.A., et al.: CredChain: academic and professional certificate verification system using blockchain. Proc. IEEE iCACCESS (2024). https://doi.org/10.1109/iCACCESS61735.2024.10499520
44. A. Tepelidis et al.: BlockAdemiC: a digital distributed verification system for educational activities in higher education. ACM DLT **4**(3) (2025). https://doi.org/10.1145/3703463
45. John, S., Hürten, M.: Implementing european digital credentials in non-formal education. In: Proc. CSEDU 2025. SciTePress (2025)
46. Tan, E., et al.: Verification of education credentials on EBSI: action research in a cross-border use case. Big Data Cogn. Comput. **7**(2), 79 (2023). https://doi.org/10.3390/bdcc7020079
47. Gamma, E., Helm, R., Johnson, R., Vlissides, J.: Design Patterns: Elements of Reusable Object-Oriented Software, Addison-Wesley (1994)
48. Mikroyannidis, A., Third, A., Domingue, J.: Blockchain-based decentralised micro-accreditation for lifelong learning. Interact. Learn. Environ. **33**(3), 2201–2215 (2024). https://doi.org/10.1080/10494820.2024.2401485
49. zkSync, zkSync Era Documentation, Matter Labs (2024). https://docs.zksync.io/
50. Tanim, A.M., Hossain, M.F., Saria, H., Mansoor, N.: Design and development of a blockchain-enabled decentralized framework for academic microcredentials, IET Softw. **2026**, article number 7326873 (2026). https://doi.org/10.1049/sfw2/7326873

# Short Paper Track

# On Shadow Impacts of Blockchain-Based Transparency Implementation for Trustworthy AI

Zheng Li[1](✉) and Yan Liu[2]

[1] Queen's University Belfast, Belfast BT9 5AF, UK
zheng.li@qub.ac.uk
[2] Concordia University, Montreal, QC H3G 1M8, Canada
yan.liu@concordia.ca

**Abstract.** Trustworthy AI (TAI) aims to address the concerns about misbehaviour and misuse of AI systems. Among the major components of AI trustworthiness, transparency is considered a first-class aspect in theory, and blockchain technologies are advocated for implementing transparency in practice. When it comes to blockchain-based transparency implementation, we notice that in addition to the immediate software/hardware expenses and labour costs related to AI systems, there are also long-lasting, indirect and even hidden consequences related to the society, economy and environment. Drawing inspiration from the other disciplines' research in shadow impacts, we also suggest defining "shadow impacts" to represent and organise various types of hidden effects in the TAI domain, so as to leverage available shadow analysis methods to systematically investigate, measure and mitigate the shadow impacts of TAI. To demonstrate and justify this newly introduced concept, we have identified a set of shadow impacts of blockchain-based transparency implementation via critical reflection together with extensive literature review. This current work plays a fundamental role in enabling quantitative shadow analysis and impact modelling, towards implementing more responsible trustworthiness in/for AI systems.

**Keywords:** Data transparency · Hidden effects · Model transparency · Responsible AI · Shadow impacts · Trustworthy AI

## 1 Introduction

Trustworthy AI (TAI) is promoted to address the increasing concerns about misbehaviour and misuse of AI systems, by making AI lawful, ethical and robust throughout the entire system lifecycle [18], and by ensuring human trust in how, when and why an AI system is developed and used. In addition to the holistic emphasis on TAI, it is also important to understand different aspects of AI trustworthiness, such as fairness, transparency, accountability, privacy,


H. Huang et al. (Eds.): ICBC 2026, LNCS 16959, pp. 101–110, 2027.
https://doi.org/10.1007/978-3-032-36766-2_7

controllability, etc. Considering that transparency "was introduced as a first-class concept in computing" decades ago [33], we have particularly focused on the transparency aspect of TAI; and considering that blockchain technologies offer capabilities of transparency, traceability and immutability [44], we have been working on blockchain-based transparency implementation for TAI.

However, as regulated by the "No-Free-Lunch" theorem, there are both direct costs and hidden effects of transparency implementation for TAI, not to mention the indirect overhead after employing blockchain technologies (e.g., the possibly massive carbon footprint [16]). Compared to the immediately visible costs related to AI systems, it is particularly crucial and valuable to proactively reveal, measure and mitigate those hidden, long-lasting, indirect effects corresponding to the social, economic, and environmental concerns.

Therefore, we have unfolded research in hidden effect analysis along with our current work on blockchain-based transparency implementation. When it comes to consistently representing and systematically summarising various types of hidden effects, we decided to resort to the concept "shadow impacts" in other disciplines, which further allows us to leverage available shadow analysis methods (e.g., the input-output model [36]) to quantitatively investigate the inter-dependencies between different factors (and their impacts) in blockchain-based transparency implementation.

To avoid losing focus, this paper mainly reports our forward-looking vision on introducing the concept "shadow impacts" to the TAI domain. To help demonstrate and justify this newly introduced concept (see Sect. 2), we have conducted critical reflection [29] together with extensive literature review, and then identified a set of typical shadow impacts of TAI with regard to implementing data transparency (see Sect. 3), implementing model transparency (see Sect. 4), and employing blockchain technologies (see Sect. 5) respectively. Correspondingly, this paper makes two main contributions:

- For researchers, the awareness of and emphasis on shadow impacts of TAI essentially broaden the spectrum of responsible AI, which creates new research and development opportunities for strengthening AI guardrails.
- For practitioners, the introduction of "shadow impacts" will enable more comprehensive cost-benefit analyses for and will bring interdisciplinary toolsets to implementing more responsible trustworthiness in/for AI systems.

## 2 Defining Shadow Impact of Trustworthy AI

The traditional and intuitive definition of shadow impact (or shadowing effect) can be found in the urban planning domain where sunlight and shadows are treated as "*a dynamic duo that not only impacts the structural and aesthetic elements of buildings but also shapes the social fabric of urban environments*" [39]. On the one hand, sunlight access is critical for maintaining a healthy living environment, with a multitude of well-known benefits for human beings (e.g., addressing vitamin D deficiencies) [14]. On the other hand, the by-products of sunlight interacting with physical urban structures, namely shadows, can negatively impact human living environments, reduce buildings' energy efficiency, and/or lower the economic value of land [26].

In addition to analysing shadow impacts in the physical sense, the concept "shadow impact" has also been adapted to and employed in many other contexts. For example, by arguing that the production, consumption and disposal of any product can place burdens on the environment, Environmental Science follows a lifecycle thinking to define shadow impacts as the hidden, often unquantified and unaccounted, indirect environmental consequences of products, activities and systems [23]. Similarly, by augmenting conventional financial metrics with carbon footprint concerns, Finance refers to shadow impacts of an investment portfolio as the economic, social and environmental effects underlying an investor's decision to place their funds in particular financial instruments [36].

Drawing inspiration from the research in shadow impacts in Finance and Environmental Science, here we also advocate the lifecycle thinking and define ***shadow impacts*** of TAI as **the hidden, unintended, and indirect effects (with respect to social, economic, and environmental concerns) behind trustworthiness implementation in/for AI systems**. Driven by our current research needs, we further narrow down the context of shadow impacts to be blockchain-based transparency implementation. Since the transparency in TAI includes both data transparency and model transparency, firstly, we distinguish the technology-agnostic shadow sources between data transparency implementation and model transparency implementation. Then, we highlight the employment of blockchain as a technological shadow source, to facilitate discussing generic shadow impacts in both cases. Different shadow sources' respective shadow impacts are exemplified in the following sections.

## 3 Shadow Impacts of Data Transparency

Data transparency, as defined as "*the ability of a subject to effectively gain access to all information related to data used in processes and decisions that affect the subject*" [13], is one of the widely recognised trustworthy dimensions of TAI [9]. It has been identified that knowing what are in the datasets and how they are used is vitally important for relevant stakeholders to dispel doubts about, and even address biases in, AI systems [22]. For example, the openness of training and fine-tuning data would allow legal professionals and the public to assess whether AI algorithms and models have ingested personal data or copyrighted materials.

To help realise data transparency and traceability for AI systems, it has been advocated to store all relevant AI data (and especially the training data) and make the data indelible [12]. This strategy, nevertheless, will lead to a wide range of negative effects, as discussed in the following subsections. It should be noted that those negative effects essentially stem from this technology-agnostic strategy, while blockchain is a candidate technology for the strategy implementation.

### 3.1 Extra Storage Overhead

Although storing everything seems to be a convenient approach to data transparency, this has been identified as "a habit that can quietly chip away at budgets, performance, and even sustainability goals" [1]. In the context of traditional applications involving large and ever growing databases, there is always an operational distinction between hot/current data and cold/historical data, and some data can eventually become inaccurate or outdated/useless to the database applications [40]. For organisations, such aged and stale data will inevitably slow down business decision making and incur monetary waste for unnecessary data storage and management [30].

The similar situations also exist in the context of AI systems. Take training data for example, not all the AI applications are designed to train models all at once and once for all. In special application scenarios that involve online machine learning, the training process can even take place continuously and/or incrementally, with one or more sliding time windows on a stream of data points in real-time. In such cases, there are little practical benefits from persistently storing outdated and stale data, and what is even worse is that the accidental use of stale data may cause irreparable damage/loss in life-critical and high-risk environments [24].

Despite those accidental consequences, immutably storing stale data on a blockchain would amplify the storage overhead of data transparency implementation. Given the full-replication data storage mechanism in the existing blockchain technologies, the copying of stale data at each node will increase overall storage per block and eventually worsen the scalability problem [35]. In other words, the realisation of blockchain-based data transparency may always have a significant side effect in terms of extra storage usage and costs. Accordingly, we consider *(extra) storage overhead* the most typical shadow impact of blockchain-based TAI with respect to data transparency implementation.

### 3.2 Privacy Risks and Legislation Violation Risks

By definition [13], data transparency in TAI requires information disclosure to improve trust in AI systems. However, a general consensus in normal life is that the more information people share and/or store, the more privacy risks they will have to take [27]. When it comes to the blockchain-based data transparency implementation, publishing all data would not only be cumbersome and expensive but may also raise additional privacy and cybersecurity risks [31], because everyone can reach the data on the ledger of an open (and especially public) blockchain platform, resulting in the disclosure of private user data (if any) [43].

In fact, data privacy is another foundational pillar of TAI. Firstly, given the fact that big data act as the fundamental fuel to the recent AI wave, building and using modern AI systems may inadvertently involve copyrighted, confidential or personal information [20]. Secondly, by collecting, analysing, and interpreting vast amounts of data, AI algorithms may be able to identify or reveal sensitive patterns about certain individuals or groups [17]. As a result, the handling of sensitive and private data has become a growing public concern about AI [3].

To protect public privacy and to regulate organisations' practices, many countries have released regulatory compliance requirements, policies and laws. Despite the criticisms about some oppressive, anti-business, and intimidating requirements of such legislations [25], blockchain technologies have inherent drawbacks against these legal frameworks. For example, although blockchain-aided TAI can be transparent about what data are collected from where and how the data are used and accessed by whom, the immutability feature of blockchain could still violate the GDPR clause "*right to be forgotten*", especially when data need to be erased.

Therefore, we consider *privacy risks* and privacy-related *legislation violation risks* as two types of shadow impacts of blockchain-based transparency implementation for TAI.

### 3.3 Extra Computation Overhead and Inevitable Transparency Compromise Due to Data Privacy Preservation

The existence of privacy risks and legislation violation risks does not mean that blockchain technologies are incorrigibly unsuitable for TAI. To relieve privacy concerns in blockchain-based data transparency implementation, researchers have proposed various privacy-preserving techniques, focusing either on data or on blockchain itself.

From the data's perspective, the general strategy is to preprocess data into some privacy-friendly formats before storing them on a blockchain. According to the literature, there are three popular types of privacy-preserving mechanisms for data, namely 1) **Data Encryption** that keeps sensitive information private and encrypted for users who have the access/operation rights and the decryption keys; 2) **Data Perturbation** that hides original information from the raw data by intentionally injecting randomisation noise; and 3) **De-identification** (or **anonymisation**) that sanitises data through generalisation and suppression before releasing the data for analytics. Unfortunately, data encryption and decryption inevitably increase the computational overhead and time cost for data processing, while multitudinous perturbation and anonymisation can sacrifice data utility and contravene data integrity, eventually leading to a compromise of data transparency.

When switching the focus to blockchain, the basic tactic is to renovate the existing blockchain technologies to improve blockchain's compatibility and compliance with privacy needs and legislations. For example, 1) the most straightforward idea is to change blockchain's visibility by distinguishing between permissionless (public) and permissioned (private or consortium) blockchains [43]; 2) the most ambitious proposal is to completely redesign blockchain and allow data to be removed from a chain [19], although this seems to have conceptually broken the blockchain protocols; 3) while the others are generally compromise solutions that allow data changes in blocks and retain the structure of current blockchain designs [21], e.g., using a *trapdoor* to modify transaction without changing its hash checksum [6]. Nevertheless, both visibility control over and data removal from a blockchain essentially indicate less information disclosure, i.e. lower data transparency.

It is known that different aspects of TAI can have frictional effects and trade-off implications on each other [2], and clearly, transparency and privacy are a pair of such aspects in this context. Considering that their mutual frictional effects can naturally fit in the predefined concept "shadow impacts" (i.e. unintended and indirect effects, see Sect. 2), by emphasising data transparency, here we recognise *(extra) computation overhead* and *(inevitable) transparency compromise* as two types of shadow impacts of blockchain-based TAI due to data privacy preservation.

## 4 Shadow Impacts of Model Transparency

Model transparency refers to the clarity and openness of AI models, indicating that an AI model's external functionalities and internal decision-making process together with its structure and parameters shall be accessible and interpretable to all stakeholders, ranging from developers to end-users [32]. It is evident that transparency in AI models directly contributes to the trustworthiness of AI systems, as users' understanding and competence can be significantly influential on the amount of trust placed upon an automated system [34]. And similar to data transparency, model transparency is also necessary and crucial for addressing those regulatory compliance and ethical considerations.

By treating model parameters and structure information as special data of AI systems, researchers have suggested using the same technology-agnostic strategy to realise both data transparency and model transparency, and blockchain has been a popular technology for the strategy implementation. For example, after training or optimising machine learning models locally, the model parameters can be immutably stored on a blockchain for transparent, credible and secure parameter/model sharing in federated learning [42] or collaborative learning [41]. Naturally, such model transparency implementations also encounter the same shadow impacts as those discussed regarding data transparency (see Sect. 3).

However, model transparency requires not only AI models' public availability (in terms of internal information and source artifacts) but also their explainability or interpretability (in terms of working mechanism and decision-marking process) [7]. The aforementioned approaches to storing/disclosing models' source data only reflect the considerations about public availability. Thus, to avoid duplication, in this section we mainly highlight the shadow impact of making AI models explainable.

### 4.1 Overall Explanation Overhead

Recall that explainability is a crucial, integral part of transparency [10], aiming to enable humans to understand, interact with, and effectively oversee AI systems especially in those high-stakes domains, such as healthcare, finance, and autonomous driving. At the legislation level, AI predictions are now required to be not only accurate but also interpretable, e.g., by the EU AI Act and the GDPR's "right to explanation". Correspondingly, various explanation mechanisms have been proposed and developed [37], ranging from explaining individual model behaviours to explaining overall prediction policies.

On the other hand, the explainability of AI systems usually introduces a hidden operational burden [15]; and to ensure reproducibility and compliance with legislations, AI systems often preserve explanation artifacts—such as intermediate models, checkpoints, attribution maps, and logs—without assessing their actual utility or distinguishing between different stakeholders' needs. These artifacts frequently overlap in informational content, yet persist across the system lifecycle, consuming storage, compute, and maintenance resources. The unwanted accumulation of redundant artifacts would lead to inflated pipelines, reduced maintainability, and increased sustainability costs.

In our recent work, we have built up testbed AI systems to quantitatively investigate different causal connections between model explainability and its costs [28]. Here, for the purpose of conciseness, we treat different types of explanation costs as a whole and define *overall explanation overhead* as a dedicated type of shadow impacts of implementing (blockchain-based) model transparency.

## 5 Shadow Impacts of Blockchain Technologies

Although offering unique features, blockchain technologies also have well-known limitations (e.g., significant upfront expense and inefficient scalability) [4]. Some of the limitations can inevitably lead to shadow impacts as long as blockchain technologies are employed, no matter for transparency implementation or for any other purpose. As a demonstration of technological shadow impacts, we briefly discuss two representative side-effects of employing blockchain, namely *(extra) communication overhead* and *(high) energy consumption*.

### 5.1 Extra Communication Overhead in Blockchain Network

To guarantee the success of transaction recording, blockchain employs a peer-to-peer (P2P) network and a suitable consensus mechanism to broadcast and synchronise data across all the peer nodes. Unfortunately, this P2P-based data flooding mechanism inevitably causes serious network congestion and inefficient bandwidth use, especially when the number of blockchain nodes increases [11]. This inefficient network communication, in addition to the inherent time complexity of consensus algorithms, significantly contributes to blockchain's scalability issues and limited transaction processing capacity [4]. Although potential solutions have been proposed to relieve network congestion to improve the scalability of blockchain [5], the efforts on integrating those solutions can still be regarded as extra overhead, for making blockchain's network communication more efficient.

### 5.2 High Energy Consumption of Blockchain Technologies

Blockchain technologies are known to be energy-hungry purposefully by design. The two main power-consumption components of a blockchain includes 1) its consensus mechanism that verifies the validity of transactions and 2) the redundant execution of transactions that verifies signatures and update state transitions in the local database of each peer node [38]. Particularly, the consensus mechanisms are generally the root cause of blockchains' enormous energy consumption, due to their heavyweight computation load (e.g., solving complex puzzles). Although alternative consensus mechanisms are being developed [8], it is foreseeable that the energy-hungry nature of blockchain networks would not be changed disruptively at least in the near future, and thus the increasing popularity of blockchain technologies would still be a serious threat to the global efforts on mitigating greenhouse gas emissions.

## 6 Conclusions and Future Work

Despite the promising potential of TAI in theory, the trustworthiness in/for AI systems comes with both visible costs and hidden effects in practice. Inspired by shadow analysis in Finance and Environment Science, we argue to adopt interdisciplinary research methods to investigate TAI's hidden effects as shadow impacts. By focusing on the transparency aspect of TAI, we have identified a set of shadow impacts of blockchain-based transparency implementation, which fundamentally enables quantitative shadow analysis and impact modelling (e.g., [28]) towards implementing more responsible (transparency in) TAI. For example, the previously discussed storage overhead, computation overhead, and communication overhead can all be quantitatively modelled into carbon footprints.

Our future work will then be unfolded along two directions. Firstly, we will keep exploring the shadow impacts of transparency and other aspects of TAI, targeting a systematic and hierarchical shadow impact framework (for locating and classifying shadow impacts). Secondly, we will conduct case studies on shadow analysis of TAI, by adopting and adapting available interdisciplinary research methods (for measuring and mitigating shadow impacts).

**Acknowledgements.** This research is supported in part by the Engineering and Physical Sciences Research Council (EPSRC) of UK Research and Innovation (UKRI) under Grant EP/Y028813/1.

**Disclosure of Interests.** The authors have no competing interests to declare that are relevant to the content of this article.

## References

1. Acquisition International: The hidden cost of overuse and misuse of data storage. https://www.acquisition-international.com/the-hidden-cost-of-overuse-and-misuse-of-data-storage/ (6 Aug 2025)

2. Agarwal, S.: Trade-Offs between Fairness, Interpretability, and Privacy in Machine Learning. Master's thesis, University of Waterloo, Waterloo, Ontario, Canada (May 2020)
3. Alamäki, A., Mäki, M., Ratnayake, R.M.C.: Privacy concern, data quality and trustworthiness of AI-analytics. In: Proc. Fake Intell. Online Summit 2019, 7 May, pp. 37–42. Satakunta University of Applied Sciences, Pori, Finland (2019)
4. Alghamdi, T.A., Khalid, R., Javaid, N.: A survey of blockchain based systems: scalability issues and solutions, applications and future challenges. IEEE Access **12**, 79626–79651 (2024)
5. Antwi, R., et al.: A survey on network optimization techniques for blockchain systems. Algorithms **15**(6), art. no. 193 (2022)
6. Ateniese, G., et al.: Redactable blockchain – or – rewriting history in bitcoin and friends. In: Proc. EuroS&P 2017, 26-28 Apr, pp. 111–126. IEEE Computer Society, Paris, France (2017)
7. Aula, V., Erkkilä, T.: AI and transparency. In: Handbook on Public Policy and Artificial Intelligence, chap. 13, pp. 170–180. Edward Elgar Publishing, Cheltenham, UK (Jun 2024)
8. Bada, A.O., et al.: Towards a green blockchain: a review of consensus mechanisms and their energy consumption. In: Proc. DCOSS 2021, 14-16 Jul, pp. 503–511. IEEE Press, Pafos, Cyprus (2021)
9. Balahur-Dobrescu, A., et al.: Data quality requirements for inclusive, non-biased and trustworthy AI. Publications Office of the European Union, Luxembourg (Dec 2022), JRC131097
10. Balasubramaniam, N.: Transparency and explainability of AI systems: from ethical guidelines to requirements. Inf. Softw. Technol. 159, art. no. 107197 (2023)
11. Berendea, N., et al.: Fair and efficient gossip in hyperledger fabric. In: Proc. ICDCS 2020, 29 Nov - 01 Dec, pp. 190–200. IEEE Press, Singapore (2020)
12. Bertino, E., Kundu, A., Sura, Z.: Data transparency with blockchain and AI ethics. J. Data Inf. Qual. **11**(4), art. no. 16 (2019)
13. Bertino, E., et al.: Redefining data transparency: a multidimensional approach. Comput. **52**(1), 16–26 (2019)
14. Bronin, S.C.: Solar rights. Boston Univ. Law Rev. **89**(4), 1217–1265 (2009)
15. Corona, J., et al.: From black box to transparency: consistency and cost within XAI. In: Proc. GC 2024 Workshops, 08-12 Dec, pp. 1–6. IEEE Press, Cape Town, South Africa (2024)
16. Digiconomist: Bitcoin energy consumption index (Dec 2025). https://digiconomist.net/bitcoin-energy-consumption
17. ELN: The future of AI privacy: What you need to know (2025). https://elnevents.com/the-future-of-ai-privacy-what-you-need-to-know
18. European Commission: Ethics guidelines for trustworthy ai (08 April 2019). https://digital-strategy.ec.europa.eu/en/library/ethics-guidelines-trustworthy-ai
19. Farshid, S., Reitz, A., Roßbach, P.: Design of a forgetting blockchain: a possible way to accomplish GDPR compatibility. In: Proc. HICSS 2019, 8-11 Jan, pp. 7087–7095. ScholarSpace, Hawaii, USA (2019)
20. Feretzakis, G., Verykios, V.S.: Trustworthy AI: securing sensitive data in large language models. AI **5**(4), 2773–2800 (2024)
21. Godyn, M.: Analysis of solutions for a blockchain compliance with GDPR. Sci. Rep. **12**, art. no. 15021 (2022)
22. Hardinges, J., Simperl, E., Shadbolt, N.: We must fix the lack of transparency around the data used to train foundation models. Harvard Data Sci. Rev. (Special Issue 5) (2024)

23. Heiskanen, E.: Every product casts a shadow: but can we see it, and can we act on it? Environ. Sci. Policy **2**(1), 61–74 (1999)
24. Holt, C., Calhoun, J.C.: Stale data analysis in intelligent transportation platooning models. In: Proc. UEMCON 2022, 26-29 Oct, pp. 0313–0320. IEEE Press, New York (2022)
25. Katulić, T.: Towards the trustworthy AI: insights from the regulations on data protection and information security. Media Res.: Croatian J. Journalism Media **26**(2), 9–28 (2020)
26. Lau, K., Ng, E., He, Z.: Residents' preference of solar access in high-density subtropical cities. Sol. Energy **85**(9), 1878–1890 (2011)
27. Li, Z., Pino, E.J.: D&D: a distributed and disposable approach to privacy preserving data analytics in user-centric healthcare. In: Proc. SOCA 2019, 18-21 Nov, pp. 176–183. IEEE Computer Society, Kaohsiung, Taiwan (2019)
28. Liu, Y., Huang, J., Hamou-Lhadj, W., Li, Z.: Redundancy as the shadow of explainability: a trade-off principle for ai-intensive systems. In: Proc. ICSE 2026, pp. 12–18. ACM Press, Rio de Janeiro, Brazil (2026) to appear
29. Lundgren, H., Poell, R.F.: On critical reflection: a review of Mezirow's theory and its operationalization. Hum. Resour. Dev. Rev. **15**(1), 3–28 (2016)
30. Magaji, J.: Data waste: What causes it and how to reduce it (2025). https://www.acceldata.io/blog/data-waste
31. Matulionyte, R., et al.: Data transparency and copyright: opportunities and challenges (Oct 2025). https://ssrn.com/abstract=5629050
32. Milvus: What is model transparency and how does it relate to Explainable AI? (Dec 2025). https://milvus.io/ai-quick-reference/what-is-model-transparency-and-how-does-it-relate-to-explainable-ai
33. Ofem, P., Isong, B., Lugayizi, F.: On the concept of transparency: a systematic literature review. IEEE Access **10**, 89887–89914 (2022)
34. Papantonis, I., Belle, V.: Model transparency: why do we care? In: Proc. ICAART 2023, 22-24 Feb, vol. 3, pp. 650–657. SCITEPRESS, Lisbon, Portugal (2023)
35. Qi, X., et al.: A reliable storage partition for permissioned blockchain. IEEE Trans. Knowl. Data Eng. **33**(1), 14–27 (2021)
36. Ritchie, J., Dowlatabadi, H.: Understanding the shadow impacts of investment and divestment decisions: adapting economic input–output models to calculate biophysical factors of financial returns. Ecol. Econ. **106**, 132–140 (2014)
37. Schwalbe, G., Finzel, B.: A comprehensive taxonomy for explainable artificial intelligence: a systematic survey of surveys on methods and concepts. Data Min. Knowl. Dis. **38**(5), 3043–3101 (2024)
38. Sedlmeir, J., et al.: Ein blick auf aktuelle entwicklungen bei blockchains und deren auswirkungen auf den energieverbrauch. Inf. Spektrum **43**(6), 391–404 (2020)
39. Singh, M.P., et al.: Architecture and sciography – the role of light and shadows. J. Eng. Tech. Manage. - JET-M **77**, 982–992 (2025)
40. Skyt, J., Jensen, C.S.: Persistent views–a mechanism for managing ageing data. Comput. J. **45**(5), 481–493 (2002)
41. Tang, X., et al.: Secure and trusted collaborative learning based on blockchain for artificial intelligence of things. IEEE Wireless Commun. **29**(3), 14–22 (2022)
42. Wang, R.: The applications of blockchain in artificial intelligence. Secur. Commun. Netw 2021, art. no. 6126247 (2021)
43. Wasim Ahmad, R., et al.: Blockchain for aerospace and defense: opportunities and open research challenges. Comput. Ind. Eng. **151**, 106982 (2021)
44. Zhang, P., Ding, S., Zhao, Q.: Exploiting blockchain to make AI trustworthy: a software development lifecycle view. ACM Comput. Surv. **56**(7), art. no. 163 (2024)

# Author Index





H. Huang et al. (Eds.): ICBC 2026, LNCS 16959, p. 111, 2027.
https://doi.org/10.1007/978-3-032-36766-2

GPSR Compliance
The European Union's (EU) General Product Safety Regulation (GPSR) is a set of rules that requires consumer products to be safe and our obligations to ensure this.

If you have any concerns about our products, you can contact us on

ProductSafety@springernature.com

In case Publisher is established outside the EU, the EU authorized representative is:

Springer Nature Customer Service Center GmbH
Europaplatz 3
69115 Heidelberg, Germany

www.ingramcontent.com/pod-product-compliance
Ingram Content Group UK Ltd.
Pitfield, Milton Keynes, MK11 3LW, UK
UKHW020148290926
15471UKWH00004B/754
*9783032367655*